Photograph by Hoover Art Studios

CARRIE JACOBS-BOND

The Roads of Melody

BY

CARRIE JACOBS-BOND

AUTHOR OF "THE END OF A PERFECT DAY"

D. Appleton and Company

New York : London

Mcmxxvii

7526

PREFACE

It would be difficult to devise a gesture more unnecessary than introducing Carrie Jacobs-Bond to a public which knows her songs by heart—and keeps them there.

In her instance, the wontedly uncertain winds of popularity have fused into a gentle, steady breeze which has blown her ballads, literally, to the uttermost parts of the earth. Where they have lodged they have remained. Only true heart songs do that. Mrs. Bond has written no other sort.

Although this is the first complete telling of her life story, it will have a familiar flavor to thousands. For into her lyrics and music, from the beginning, she has woven easily identifiable fragments of that story. It may be a shred of simple philosophy, a hint of her own real courage, a flash of serene faith, the warm glow of her love for flowers and sunsets and human beings—

v

but, inevitably, the fragment is there. It is an authentic fragment. Mrs. Bond can interpret only a mood in which she believes.

Hence, since brief foreword is deemed desirable, it is fitting that this should be attempted by one of the average audience that she has reached. Avowedly, Mrs. Bond has written for the average man and woman. She has us in mind, far more than David Bispham, Evan Williams, Jessie Bartlett Davis and the rest of the lovely voices which first spread the Bond tradition.

The mode of the moment bids us shun sentimentality. Yet we average folk, whether or no we deny it, are incurably sentimental. Uttering unsophisticated affection for God, nature, sweetheart, child, friend or native land calls for bravery—in 1927. All this is going out of fashion, if our glib critics of manners and customs may be relied upon. We average folk, bewildered, find ourselves enmeshed in glittering phrase-nets. More than once a song of Carrie Jacobs-Bond has set us free, has revealed the net as a tangle of rotten threads twisted in Lilliputia.

Let us hold, then, a brief for sentimentality:

Preface

By the right of recalling starlight over an Adirondack lake; the faint drip from your paddle blade, the embers of a dying camp fire ahead, and, from the screening tamaracks of Indian Bay, a contralto voice. That was how we first heard "A Perfect Day."

In the name of the legions who have listened to "I Love You Truly," with, perhaps, the gentle creak of a Nantucket porch hammock between stanzas and the soft nimbus of a piano lamp upon the hair of the one You the song seemed written for.

By the memory of "Just a-Wearyin' for You" —Frank Stanton's words, set to a melody that clutched then and still clutches. That singer sings no more, and only the other day Stanton ceased verse-making forever. But, being an average human being, we go on remembering.

Sentimentality wears well, when it is honest sentimentality. Mrs. Bond's life has proved it.

Robert Emmet MacAlarney.

Green Hill Farms,
Overbrook, Pennsylvania.

CONTENTS

ILLUSTRATIONS

Illustrations

The ROADS OF MELODY

CHAPTER I

EARLY STRUGGLES

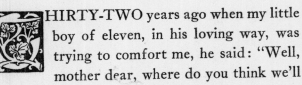 HIRTY-TWO years ago when my little boy of eleven, in his loving way, was trying to comfort me, he said: "Well, mother dear, where do you think we'll be a year from to-night?" little dreaming of the terror his words brought me as I looked into the future. But, answering him smilingly, I told him the most fantastic fairy story. I don't remember now what it was about but it might just as well have been this.

"If you had said, say, thirty-five years from to-night, darling, I could tell you just as well! And so, I think, thirty-five years from to-night I shall have to my credit two hundred or more little songs which are out in the world working for us among all English-speaking folk, and knocking at the door of foreign lands for translation. They will have earned for us a lovely home on a hillside in Hollywood, California, with a little nest in San Diego; and I shall be sitting at a desk in the Warburton House in Philadelphia, writing the story of my life. And all because I started a business with 'Belief in Hope' as my only asset.

"You will be a man, my partner, my best friend, and my pal, and we shall have all the things we wish for—but that will be easy, for you and I love simple things."

All this might have been said as my little boy and I sat in our simple home at Janesville, Wisconsin, among the treasures of our past happiness, clasping each other's hands and wondering what the future was going to bring.

The only thing that seems to me at all remarkable about my life is that I was nearly thirty-two years old before I ever even thought of having a career. In Janesville, Wisconsin, where I was born in 1862, I was early given some instruction in music and painting, but anything that I could turn to in case of need was not taught me. It was the necessity of supporting myself and my little son that made me a writer of songs. It is true that even as a little girl, when I thought of the future, I always thought of myself as a song writer; in fact, I think that some of the most beautiful music I have ever known was music that I imagined I heard in those childhood days. And even now, when I am quiet, I hear exquisite music that is all too lovely and too beautiful to try to play. I could not play it even if I desired to do so. I have no doubt that other people who love certain things deeply see or hear them in their imagination. I think every one who paints a great picture has the outline in his imagination long before he touches the brush, and that there are many wonderful pictures he never paints.

I like to cherish the belief that I had a greater talent than the world knows anything about, but a few years ago, any doubts or misgivings on that score were swept away in a satisfaction that came to me. It was when I had become a little tired of hearing "The End of a Perfect Day" sung and played. Suddenly it became a song of glory to my heart. "The End of a Perfect Day" was published, I suppose, at a psychological moment,

3

and it was very well known when the War was declared. The boys began singing it in the camps themselves and whenever I went to a camp the first thing they would ask of me was to sing "The End of a Perfect Day" for them. Often when I had done so they would ask me to sing it again and anywhere from three to ten thousand soldiers would join in and sing with me. It was then that I felt glad to be a writer of home songs and songs that touch the heart, rather than a great musician, after all.

In the lobby of the Davis House, a hotel that my grandfather owned in Janesville, I overheard a little girl say one day many years ago: "Well, Carrie Jacobs was born with a silver spoon in her mouth." I had occasion to remember this many times in the years that followed, for the things that happened to me did not seem to have much that was silver about them. I don't know what happened, but I recall feeling all around the inside of my mouth, and very thoughtfully concluding finally that it was gone—I must have swallowed it.

But my little friend was right about having it to begin with, for in childhood I did seem to have

4

Where I Was Born

DR. HANNIBAL C. JACOBS, MY FATHER

MY MOTHER

everything. I was surrounded by a loving mother, father, grandparents, aunts and uncles. My people lived on fifteen lovely acres about three miles outside of the little town. There was a charming apple orchard and beautiful arbors for the grapevines and wonderful places to roam about; gardens where there were flowers and gardens where all the vegetables were planted. My grandfather's house was a beautiful square brick place with a cupola. I used to tell the children that I was born up there. I was severely reprimanded for this, and I sometimes wonder now, when I hear my friends correcting their children for what are known as fibs, whether or not it is a wise policy. These deviations from the truth are sometimes the sign of imagination. That I was born in that cupola I really believed, for to me it was the most interesting and the nicest part of the house.

In the grounds was a small square brick building, which was used for a smoke house, and I often wondered why grandfather didn't give it to me for a playhouse. But what was the use of gardens and grapevines, if the soil could be made to grow tobacco? And so this beautiful place of

5

my grandfather's was sold and made into a tobacco farm. The lovely old brick house, once so far out in the country but now within the town, still stands. Only a few years ago the citizens of Janesville put a tablet on it marking it as the place of my birth.

When I was four years old, I suddenly discovered that I could pick out airs on the piano with one finger, and my father and mother would take turns singing or whistling tunes for me to play. By the time I was six years old, I could play almost anything by ear and always with a good accompaniment. At seven almost any one at all would have recognized what I was playing. My father appreciated, and I think understood, this musical talent better than any one else. When I was nine, I could play Liszt's Second Hungarian Rhapsody entirely by ear, accurately enough for persons familiar with the composition to recognize it. Five years later I went with Frank L. Bond (who many years later was to be my husband) to Myers Opera House to hear Madame Julia Reeve King, a very fine pianist. That evening was the first time I had ever been allowed out without a member of the family. But I was even more thrilled when Madame King played Liszt's Second Hungarian Rhapsody. In those days this piece was considered a test of a performance.

At that time, had we been living in New York or some other large center, more attention would have been paid to the marked talent I had displayed. Some one would have thought of a musical education for me. I never heard an opera until I was twenty, when I heard Scalchi and Patti in "Semiramide"—a very good introduction to grand opera. It was given in the old exposition building in Chicago, then the only place large enough for such a great occasion. It was even later that I heard my first symphony played by Theodore Thomas' orchestra in the Auditorium in Chicago. And yet, though they were not trained musicians, mine was a musical family on both sides. Every one except my grandfather Davis, who could not carry a tune, played some instrument. My aunt, who did not know a note of music, composed many charming waltzes and my uncle invented a guitar and played very well upon it. Some of the loveliest music that I remember I heard my father play on a flute, which his father

7

had made for him and I still have. There was also handed down to me a carved music rack which this same grandfather made. Grandmother Jacobs' first cousin was John Howard Payne, who wrote the libretto for the opera, "Clari," that contained one number that eclipsed all else—the song "Home, Sweet Home."

Now it has been said by many persons that I am not a trained musician and that I know no music. This is untrue. I studied and studied laboriously, but the teachers I had were the sort one would find in a town like Janesville fifty years ago —just the everyday, perfectly competent and understanding, but none the less routine, music teachers. It is true that I was never taught harmony or composition. However, in the early days I did write my own manuscripts and they were perfectly intelligible; in fact, I was not a little surprised when I learned that I could do this. Later Mr. Nelson, my music printer in Chicago, found for me an excellent musician who could take down my songs from dictation. I saw no reason why I should not do that just as a novelist dictates to a stenographer. I have been told that some really well-known writers spell badly, but before one can dictate music well one should know it.

I have great reason to remember, but I suppose that there are few people to-day who do remember, a boy pianist, called Blind Tom, who traveled around the country and appeared at recitals in theaters and town halls. His parents had been slaves and his musical talent was discovered one night when there were guests for dinner at the master's house in which he and his parents were servants. One of the guests had played a very beautiful composition and then every one went into the garden and to their great astonishment this little Negro boy crept to the piano and played almost perfectly the piece that he had heard. They came in quietly from the garden to see who was playing and found the frightened Negro boy. From this time on, he was taken in hand by some one who for many years earned a considerable fortune from him, and for him. He was not considered bright, however, in any way but his music. He could play anything once he had heard it.

One December when I was eight, Blind Tom, then a man of about thirty-five, gave a concert at the Myers Opera House in Janesville. Blind

Tom's manager or some one managing the concert asked if there was any one in the audience who had an original composition which had never been published, and if so would he kindly come to the platform and play it?

Professor Titcomb, who was later my teacher, and who is now living near me in Hollywood, played a piece of his own which had never been printed, and in the midst of it, one of the men standing around the piano struck a high note of discord which no performer could have reached. I remember thinking at the time what a cruel thing it was to make that poor blind Negro hear that note of discord. Blind Tom, however, played the composition beautifully and when he came to that note which he could not reach with his hands, he leaned down to the keyboard and struck it with his nose. He impressed me then as being quite the most wonderful man in the world. And how the audience applauded him! I have forgotten who it was but some one bursting with local pride shouted amidst the confusion: "We have a little girl here, Carrie Jacobs, who can play like that."

How well I remember my father leading me to

the platform! I stood there while Blind Tom played a march that was all in octaves. It was extremely difficult for my small hands, but I played it after him and my father was very proud. It was my first appearance in public and there was quite a demonstration when I had finished. I have no idea what this march was or whether it has ever been published, but I can play it to-day. Such playing is a gift. I cannot explain it. I did not begin to take lessons until I was nearly ten years old, for it was not thought necessary for me to do so. As soon as I started to study, I began to lose this talent for playing so easily by ear. Teachers would never play a piece for me, for as soon as they did, I had learned it. For years and years I tried not to play from memory and when I started to compose, I kept away from other people's work as much as possible, as I found it too confusing.

For about eight years I worked at my lessons and in my own peculiar way was very faithful with my practicing. But often when I went to take my lessons, my teacher decided I had not been practicing correctly and that I should have to do it all over again. But there was one thing they never could accuse me of, I never played discords. Professor Titcomb often said to me: "That is very good, but I think if I were in your place I would go home and learn that piece now." I was always mortified. I wouldn't say that I enjoyed the five-finger exercises, but I learned that it was very necessary to know the proper fingering and I mastered it when very young. If the importance of such practice faithfully done was understood by young musicians, a great deal of unhappiness and anxiety might be saved later, but I never had to practice scales and trills—I could always play, but, oh! my fingering—that I fought hard to learn.

The things that have happened to me have always happened suddenly. Without warning the whole world seems to change for me. It was so when my father lost everything he had in a grain panic and died shortly thereafter. We were forced to give up our own lovely home and move to my grandfather's hotel, the Davis House. Here I was more alone than I had ever been and I spent hours at the piano. I felt somewhat of a dependent, but through no act of my dear, generous grandfather, and I tried to solve this at the age of twelve by going to work for the town milliner. I lasted just one day, for when I went home

I found that my grandfather had missed me, and being questioned, I confessed what I had done. He exploded: "I guess the men of this family will always be able to take care of our women folks."

During a great snowstorm that same winter, Joseph Jefferson came to my grandfather's hotel in Janesville to play "Rip Van Winkle," his lovable characterization which was not then so familiar as it became later. He had with him a little dog who went to Myers Opera House at night and played Schneider, in the early part of the play. The snowstorm continued and Mr. Jefferson was forced to stay at the Davis House for a week. In that time Schneider and I became devoted friends. We were inseparable and the lovable Mr. Jefferson had to use force to get the dog to leave my side. He decided that it perhaps would be better to leave him behind and Schneider was given to me. He was my friend and confidant for six years. I told him everything. I suppose I told him that I wanted to be a song writer some day, that I was going to own a home of my own and be in a place where no one would have to take care of me and that he could come there and live. Another thing I told my dog about was the character I had invented, "My Old Man."

Grandfather Davis was a very fine man but he was not the old-fashioned sort of person with whom a child could be very intimate and the original stories I invented were supposed to have been about a grandfather who took his place. Later I used this character in sketches and verses. When I found that my concert program of playing and singing my own songs did not seem varied enough, I included a recitation or two about "My Old Man." Through this character I could say things about places and people that I could not voice so well myself. In one of these recitations "My Old Man" talked of his boyhood. It was really a reflection of my own childhood and the things I loved:

The road through the Home Woods was
lovely to-day
For the rain came down in its old soft way,
Just a-pattin' the leaves as it gently fell,
A-tellin' the tales that I loved so well,
A-singin' the songs that filled me with joy,
For I lived once again the life of a boy.

Early Struggles

The same sweet smell of the balsam tree
Came floatin' by and it whispered to me,
And it said as it passed through the ferns and
  flowers,
"This takes me back to my boyhood hours,
Oh, these are the things that I used to know
And loved so well in the long ago."

Yes, I lived again my boyhood hours,
And forgot the thorns in the path of flowers,
Forgot the stones and the stubble too,
Forgot all the sad things I ever knew,
And lived once again my life of joy
And lived it just as a country boy.
Oh, the rain in the woods, and the song-bird's
  cheer!
I live it again every blessed year,
And the days that are best are the days that
  rain
And I am a happy boy again.

Life went on uneventfully for a number of
years. At eighteen I was married to Mr. E. J.
Smith. After seven years we were separated. At
twenty-five, I married Dr. Frank Lewis Bond,
who took a deep and sympathetic interest in my
music and encouraged me to put down on paper

some of the little songs that were continually running through my mind. I could play for him as I never have played for any one else, hours at a time.

With Dr. Bond, my little son and I went to live in Iron River, a small mining town in northern Michigan. Here, I spent the seven happiest years of my life. Our life there in the great pine forests was almost idyllic.

But all this happiness went—again with suddenness. The iron mines closed. The doctor not only lost much money that he had invested in them, but the people he had cared for could not pay him; in fact, there had been no accounts kept. Any doctor or doctor's wife will understand how this could come about.

Being optimistic as well as a dreamer, I decided that all there was to do was to publish some of my songs, and we could move to a city and I could earn enough money to supply our needs while my husband became known and worked up a new practice, but Dr. Bond had the same ideas of women going to work when there were men in the family as my grandfather had, and our first real disagreement came on this, but he finally consented.

AT THE AGE OF EIGHT WHEN I PLAYED FOR BLIND TOM

MY MOTHER'S FAMILY

I had written down five or six songs and I felt that they were salable.

I actually thought from what I had been told about my music that the only thing necessary was for me to be heard. Now any one who knows anything about music publishing will know how absurd my idea was. As I look back, I was a brilliant case of the fool rushing in where angels fear to tread. Sometimes such people are fortunate. I was. In my innocence, I thought all that was needed to have a song known and eagerly bought was to have some slight mention made of it in a newspaper. Thus equipped with wordly wisdom, I went to the office of the Chicago *Herald* and sent in my card to Mr. Scott, the editor. He was a charming man and very sympathetic and patient. He never, in our conversation, betrayed to me that there was anything extraordinary in my request, and I told him my story and some of the things that were happening in northern Michigan. After listening an hour or so he told me to go downstairs and see a woman staff writer, who, under the name of Amber, conducted a special department of features in the *Herald*. "If you can interest Amber as you have

17

me," Mr. Scott told me, "she can have whatever space she wants to give you."

So I took my little bundle of music and went down three flights of stairs and there met a rather young woman who had the most beautiful brown eyes, the shade of amber. I knew the moment I saw her why she had taken the nom de plume of Amber. In private life she was Mrs. Holden. Among the people who then wrote for the Chicago papers, she was a great favorite and at the old Bohemian Club, which was made up almost entirely of professional people, and to which distinguished persons felt honored to be asked, she was called the Queen of Bohemia. I spent the rest of the afternoon talking to Amber, who was one of the most sympathetic persons I have ever met.

We went to Thompson's restaurant for dinner and after we talked for a long time and I had agreed to play some of my music that night at the Bohemian Club, we went to a dingy building on a side street down near the newspaper offices.

Up through a darkened building we mounted three flights and then from a dark hallway entered a dimly lighted room. Down the center of the room was a long table lighted with candles. On one end was a little beer keg and at the other a coffee urn. And this was the Bohemian Club! Gradually, people came in and I was introduced to them as they arrived. They would sit at the table in little groups, talking quietly, but by eleven o'clock the room was crowded. Eugene Field was there and he recited some of his verses. John Vance Cheney, the poet, and Grace Duffy Boylan, who was then a Chicago newspaper woman, and later one of my truest friends, were present. Dan O'Leary, the famous walker, I found very charming, and dear Opie Reed and many others whose names were better known to me in later years than they were then. The most popular member of the group that night was Ben King, who recited some verses which he said he had written that day. They were those lines:

IF I SHOULD DIE

If I should die to-night
And you should come to my cold corpse and say,
Weeping and heartsick o'er my lifeless clay—
If I should die to-night,

And you should come in deepest grief and woe—
And say: "Here's that ten dollars that I owe,"
  I might arise in my large white cravat
  And say, "What's that?"

  If I should die to-night
And you should come to my cold corpse and kneel,
Clasping my bier to show the grief you feel,
  I say, if I should die to-night
And you should come to me, and there and then
Just even hint 'bout payin' me that ten,
  I might arise the while,
  But I'd drop dead again.

Then Amber announced that she had discovered that afternoon a new composer who would play some of her own songs. I think I played for about three-quarters of an hour and everybody was most kind. Ethelbert Nevin, who was just beginning to be known, came in while I was playing. He talked to me most encouragingly. Of all the times I remember vividly, I think I recall that night more than any other. Every one was so enthusiastic that I concluded I had made a great mistake in postponing the publication of my songs so long. What that evening meant to one who had lived practically all her life in Janesville and in the great pine forest of northern Michigan!

Amber asked me the next day what I wanted to do. "You want to meet some publishers, don't you?" She arranged an appointment for me with one of the largest publishing firms in Chicago. I played over my songs and they were quite enthusiastic. They thought that I should be able to sell them, but the songs were not just what *they* were looking for. "Could you write some children's songs?"

I thought that I could and went back to the hotel where I was stopping and worked earnestly for hours. At last I produced some verses called, "Is My Dolly Dead?":

> *I dropped dolly—broke her head,*
> *Some one told me my doll's dead,*
> *Tell me, dolly, is it true,*
> *I can no more play with you?*
> *Dolly girl, whose eyes were blue,*
> *I'm your friend, I will be true.*
> *Tho' your face no more I'll see,*
> *You I've loved, you'll stay with me.*
> *Should you lose your hair as well,*
> *Just keep covered, and don't tell.*
> *Lucie Dolly, don't say no—*
> *Stay with me, I love you so.*

The Roads of Melody

Some dolls live without their eyes.
Yes, you wonder with surprise,
But I know and so do you—
Dolls with no heads live 'tis true.
Dolly girls for children poor,
Have been made of cloth I'm sure
Tied up pieces, made of rags,
Thus called dolls, yet look like bags—
Yet for playmates they will do,
Lots of children say so, too—
Love them truly, yes they do,
Just the same as I love you.

Two days later I took the verses and the music to the publisher and played the song over for them. It was accepted and we entered into an agreement that I was to receive royalty on the copies sold. Through the efforts of my new friend, Amber, the song was sung within five days by Teresa Vaughn as an encore to "Sally in Our Alley," in the popular extravaganza called "Fourteen Ninety-two." The song was most successful, and I went back to northern Michigan feeling perfectly confident of supporting the family until Dr.. Bond's plans could mature. But this dream never came true.

While my song, "Is My Dolly Dead?", was still being sung in the "Extravaganza of Fourteen Ninety-two," the whole world was again changed for me by the sudden death of Dr. Bond. The evening of this accident, as he was leaving the house to make a professional call, he turned from the door, and smilingly said, "Harder every time I say 'good-by' to you. But that's the way it should be, and always will be. We know love is the greatest thing in the world because we're lovers."

These words were burned into my heart to live forever, for a few minutes later I heard from his dying lips, "My darling, this is death. But, oh, I want to live."

As he had left the house he had met some boys and girls outside, and they were throwing snow-balls and pushing each other into the drifts. A young girl came up behind Dr. Bond and pushed him. He fell, striking a piece of frozen ground. Instantly he sensed he had been desperately hurt. He lingered five agonizing days.

The time had now passed for me to write happy children's songs, but a year later I began to write again; in the first place because I knew it would please him; and in the second place, hoping as I had always hoped, that my songs would help us.

The first little song written at this time was called "Shadows," and was later published in *The Book of Seven Songs.* I quote here:

Once more I sit at evening and watch the embers burn,
The shadows all come creeping around me as I turn,
And then I see a sweet face, from which all care has gone
That sets my soul to dreaming of old times, love and song.

I know you're way off yonder, but still you seem with me,
And through the evening shadows your form I almost see.
I almost hear you whisper these words, "I love but you,
And soon we'll be united, sweetheart, be brave, be true!"

And later this little song, as yet unpublished:

Way down the road of happy years
Through lights of happy days
I seem to see your face aglow
Through all the golden rays.

Early Struggles

And through the sound of waving grass,
And through the whispering tree
I seem to hear your voice again
And you are calling ME.

Oh! Happy road of years and days,
Dear sounds of grass and tree,
I wish I were as much to you
As you have been to me.

There was four thousand dollars' life insurance. It took a little over a thousand to pay funeral expenses and bills in the little town. And so, with less than three thousand dollars, and no practical ability of any kind, I was thrown on the world with my son as well as myself to support. I had been an invalid for several years, and I was no longer young. I was at an age when most women are contentedly and complacently enjoying home life and looking forward to a tranquil future.

Though broken in health, I felt confident as I had before and I put the insurance money out at interest, for I felt that I could earn my own living with some sort of work. Moreover I had something to live for. There was Fred, my son—some one to be responsible for, some one to make happy, and some one who in later years would be my partner in business, my most adoring son and my *truest friend*.

My first thought was of Janesville, where I was born, but there was no way for me to make a living there. And so I took my furniture and moved to Chicago. I took a house near the College of Physicians and Surgeons and decided that I would rent out rooms. This is probably the origin of the newspaper story which once had some little circulation that I was born in poverty and by dint of hard work finally accumulated enough money to become a successful boarding-house keeper. I never knew enough about managing anything to run a successful boarding house; certainly it would have been better for me in those early days in Chicago if I really had been clever enough to run a boarding house. I have, however, always been glad that I made the experiment of running a rooming house. It was a wonderful experience, though not a profitable one.

Having been a doctor's wife, I was necessarily interested in the young men who were struggling so hard and making such sacrifices to earn their way through the medical college, as many of them were. A few snobs occupied my better rooms, but most of them were wonderful and kind to me, and best of all I learned much of what humanity really was. There is only one way to know people, and that is to be as poor as you can be. There are always plenty of friends on a sunny day; but when there's a bad storm and you're a rooming-house keeper, the folks that are kind to you then—that's different. I have tried to keep track of some of those men and most of them I shall never forget.

I soon reached the point, however, where I had to get back the money which I had loaned and we began to live upon the three thousand dollars. I moved into a smaller house—I believe the rent was forty dollars, and I knew no way to earn that much a month. This was in the nineties, when hand-painted china had something of a vogue, and I had been taught to do such work in Janesville. I could do passably good work and I began to sell things occasionally. I had some cards made and sent these out to a few sympathetic friends. They were glad to buy my work to give as presents. They told other people, and in time I had a few customers. Among them was a young life-insurance agent who in some way had learned my story, and from the time we met until I gave up the painting, I think my china was the only gift he ever made any one. I always had a little order in reserve from him in case times grew desperately hard. He wasn't rich, but he helped everybody to the limit of his means.

One day he came to see me, and I said, "I've written a verse about you. Want to hear it?" and laughingly I read these lines to him:

There's the life-insurance agent; there's the life-
*   insurance man.*
Do you think you can escape him? Better do it
*   if you can,*
'Cause if once he gets a-goin', might as well give
*   in, you bet!*
You never can escape him if on you his heart
*   gets set—*
*   You get insured!*

First, he tells you 'bout the money you save by
*   signing now;*
How in twenty years th' endowment takes the
*   wrinkles off your brow.*

28

Early Struggles

Pay about three dollars every month for forty
    years
May save 'bout the fourteen hundred, 'nough to
    wipe out all your fears,
       And you're insured!

But you let the good chance slip you, like as not
    you'll rue the day
When you didn't take insurance when the man
    was round your way;
For he's mighty independent, and he doesn't care
    a snap,
If the lightnin' comes and strikes you, and you're
    wiped clean off the map,
       And you ain't insured!

But without a bit of foolin', life insurance's
    mighty slick,
Twenty years just goes a scootin', get your money
    pretty quick.
And when you're dead you needn't worry, you've
    left somethin' for your wife,
Life insurance worth a thousand, there's your
    money or your life.
       You was insured!

As I read this to him, he smiled and said:
"You know, I can't give you a thousand dollars

outright, Mrs. Bond, but if you'll let me have that little poem to use, I'll keep the endowment up on a policy for you for ten years, and at the end of that time you'll get a thousand dollars. Want to do it?"

Well, I rather think I did. And sure enough, ten years later, to my great surprise I received a letter with a check for one thousand dollars that I had entirely forgotten about. If I had received that check during the time I really was in great need, the shock would probably have killed me, but it came after I was used to seeing sixty dollars a month, and while it was a wonderful surprise, I wasn't entirely overcome.

When I moved into this new house it was summer, and I had no thought of the expense of heating all its rooms in winter. I had never learned anything so practical. When winter came I had to take money from my little hoard to buy coal. As there was too much space for us to heat, we shut off the back rooms and lived entirely in the front of the house. Poor as we were and discouraging as everything was we did not have to look far that winter in Chicago to find people who were much more desperate than we were. One day a poor soul who had been walking in the snow and the sleet came to my door and said he would clean off the steps for ten cents. I thought a few moments; ten cents was ten cents even then. I wouldn't have believed that a time could come when it would seem a good deal more than ten cents. But I had to refuse, for I was not spending even ten cents for anything I could do without or for anything that we could do for ourselves. However, he was so poor looking and so pathetically cold and ragged that I asked him to come in and sit down and get warm. He sat by our fire and rubbed his thin, shaky hands together. I gave him some bread and butter, and while he was eating it I went back to the work of copying some music; for I was always writing, and the publishers who took "Is My Dolly Dead?" had accepted several more songs, but I did not seem to be making a cent of money from them.

He looked at me and said: "Madam, I can do that for you." I glanced at the cold chapped hands, and he continued: "I used to coach the glee club music at a southern college. I can do a very good manuscript." I handed him my work and I could see at once that he knew what he was doing. As though in response to a question from me which I did not ask but was merely thinking, he went on: "You see, I had a home and a good business and we were living comfortably enough, but my wife and I had a quarrel over religion and I just couldn't stand it and I walked out and never went back. Sometimes I think I'd like to do something else, but I haven't the clothes now to go into an office, and I long ago lost my courage, and we reach a point where nothing matters much, don't we?"

I did not feel that way and I told him so. "Where are you going to sleep to-night?" He didn't know, and I gave him the use of one of the back rooms. It was cold, but he didn't find it so. And there he stayed for three months, and in return for his room he brought in the coal and took out the ashes and cleaned the steps. He always left early in the morning and I suppose he just wandered the streets during the day. I took this man in because he was more unfortunate than we were. It gave me a certain courage to keep going. The worst suffering is that which comes to those who have formerly had the good things and have had to give them up, or to those who pity themselves constantly. He was never communicative after the first day and the only time I ever saw his worn, weather-beaten face really moved was the night that proved to be his last with me.

It was a stormy, bitter, dark winter night about eight o'clock. He came in excitedly to tell me that a terrible thing had happened down the alley. A poor man, his wife, and three children had been dispossessed and they and their few belongings had been set out in the snow. They could not even scrape together the little rent that was asked for the barn in which they lived. I told him to get them. As he was leaving he called to me, "They can have my room."

He brought them back. We built an extra fire for them, and did all we possibly could to make that wretched family comfortable in the quarters that had been his. And then he left, with as little explanation as when he came. I never saw him again; but one does not forget even unsung and nameless heroes, and I've often thought of him since.

The father of this family had been a drayman

but he had been informed by some chance acquaintance that if he studied hard he could take a civil-service examination and become a postman. He, it appears, was tired of riding and wished to walk—a postman's life had seemed to him almost ideal! Studying was very slow work and he made no progress at night, so he gave up his job as a drayman and the family lived on their little savings in hopes of the fine salary that Uncle Sam would pay. Alas, he failed in the examination and he lost all heart and courage and they were all in that state when they moved into my house.

The next morning when I woke up I found that fate had played another trick upon me. Suddenly—as ever—I could not move; I had a severe attack of inflammatory rheumatism. And so for four months the little family took care of me. When I was better the drayman got a job in a livery stable. He thought that they had imposed enough on my hospitality. Shortly after they moved I went to call upon them and found the man wearing one of my husband's old suits, and on their floor were two rugs which I knew had been taken from one of the boxes in the back room that we had to use for storage. I succeeded in controlling my expression for I did not want them to know that I recognized the things. I only thought how selfish I had been in keeping uselessly stored away in boxes articles that somebody else needed. Poverty was changing my whole outlook on life. Those rugs were made for use; and that man who needed the suit fitted it better than it fitted in a storage trunk. Later when I had occasion to look in that trunk I found that the moths had eaten practically all of a wonderfully warm fur coat which had belonged to my husband. No one has a right to hoard things which he cannot use.

CHAPTER II

UP THE LADDER

ONE very cold winter afternoon, as I was hurrying along Lake Park Avenue in Chicago, I passed what had once been a fine private residence; but on the lovely old door was posted a sign, "Three Rooms for $15.00." We were paying the same money for one room where we were. I went in and found three spacious rooms on the second floor. The ground floor had been converted into a restaurant, which was in charge of Miss McGraw. The three rooms for rent, on the drawing-room floor, comprised double drawing-rooms and a library; and, to make an apartment, a bathroom had been put in under the staircase. In each of the front rooms was a beautiful carved marble mantel. In what once had been a lovely library was the place to put a gas stove for cooking. It was a very convenient room with back door and porch.

Up the Ladder

This old house was at 42 East 31st Street, and as I look back to the seven years spent in it, I know they were the fullest and most important in my entire life. It was here I received an education which fitted me for almost everything that came to my life. Some people call it the University of Hard Knocks; I did not. I called it my University of Great Experience, and it was here that the inspiration for the Bond Shop was born. It was here that my son and I first became business partners, and when we left dear old No. 42 East 31st Street, it was to go to better things, where money was no longer our chief and almost our sole concern. But that is somewhat ahead of my story.

Small as this rent was, I often found it hard to meet those fifteen dollars a month, and sometimes quite impossible. This property belonged to a real estate concern called Dunlap Smith and Company, and one of their important officials was George W. Cobb, the gentleman with whom I always arranged my business, and in whom, after the first year, I confided (as much as I ever confided my troubles to any one). Often I had to tell him that it was impossible for me to pay my rent; and there was a time when I owed for six months; but the first day of every month, whether I had the money or not, I went to the office of Dunlap Smith and Company and told Mr. Cobb the truth, and he believed every word I said. I often lived on one meal a day; that seemed to be my chief idea of how to save money. The rent—that was my first concern; because I felt, if you have a roof over your head, you can always manage the rest somehow. It was true. After I lost a home and was adrift, I learned that if you can own but one room, and know it is yours, life is much more livable. The thought that somebody can put you out on the street, if you do not pay the rent, is indeed a terrible feeling. Of course my fears on this score were all imagination, as no one ever treated me badly. Always in reply to my saying that I was sorry that I had brought no rent money that day, Mr. Cobb would say, "Mrs. Bond, don't worry about the rent. I know you are going to pay it. No one ever fails who works as faithfully and hopefully as you do. Stay where you are and pay when you can. Just keep at your work."

As the weeks went by I thought: "What can I

do to reconcile myself to this life?" Then a thought came to my mind—a thought that really saved me:

"You are not the worst-off person in the world. Look around and find some one who is having a harder time than you are. There certainly are plenty of them in the world."

Scarcely had I thought that when some one rang my bell, and sure enough, there was a living demonstration—some one in more trouble than I was. He begged for just a chance to earn enough for a meal. He did not ask for any charity, he merely wanted work, the same old work of sweeping off the snow. This I let him do. He swept off the snow and I gave him a dime. But while he was still cleaning the steps I rushed down to Miss McGraw and asked her if she would give the man a cup of coffee. That was the beginning of our partnership, Miss McGraw's and mine, and this poor beggar opened the eyes of us both, I guess, to what we could do.

It was too cold now to use the kitchen. We could not afford to keep three rooms warm. And as I still had plenty of furniture stored down in the basement of this old place, I immediately made a little bedroom of the back room and for the seven years I was there, each winter I gave the little back room to some poor, starving, frozen old soul who had more troubles than I had. And out of all my experience I think that meeting with these people was perhaps the most interesting, and in some ways, the most helpful.

As time went on, some furniture and most of the silver, and nearly all of the china that I had painted for my own home, had to be sold—just a piece at a time, but after a little while it was all gone; and sometimes it looked as though I would have to sell the beautiful piano which Dr. Bond had given me for a wedding present, but like so many things we dread that never happened. I will say that many of my friends expected me to be murdered by one of those back roomers of mine. I was never afraid of this, but, as a precautionary measure, I always rolled my bed against the door after my little back roomer had gone in.

Naturally I was imposed upon at times; but it seems to me that during those days of direst poverty, I found a *camaraderie* among the poor that made them kind and honorable. This belief my son and I carried on with us in our business. We always trusted every one once; and I do not believe, in all our years of business, we have ever lost more, say, than five hundred dollars. Business men with whom I have talked say that is extraordinary, and that people dealing in music must be more honest than those dealing in other commodities. A great oil man laughingly told me once, when he heard me say this about the honesty of people, "It might work with everything else, but not with the oil station."

Now, among the poor people who came to my door, was one whom I shall never forget. One bitter, freezing, stormy night, when it seemed almost too cold for any human being to be out, the bell rang. I went to the door and there stood a shivering colored man.

"Can I just come in and get warm?" he pleaded. "I'm nearly frozen."

I looked at him and believed. I rapped on the floor. That was my signal to Miss McGraw that some one was coming down for a cup of coffee, and I took my guest in through the little back room and sent him down through the back door to Miss McGraw's back door. She and I understood each other perfectly, and the color of humanity did not make much difference to us. I had told the man that he was to come back when he had had his coffee, which he did. Then I told him he could sleep in the little back bedroom and bade him good night.

He behaved differently from my other lodgers. He did not leave the back room for three days, except to go down to Miss McGraw's kitchen and there, she said, he took only a cup of coffee—he wouldn't eat anything. Finally, we decided to give him the snow-shoveling to do, and he began to take an interest. The fifth day he declared he had been given a new lease on life, thanked us, and went away.

Five years elapsed, it was the day before Christmas, and again my little bell rang. When I answered, there was a colored man, all dressed up, looking radiantly happy.

"Why, missy," he said, "don't you know me? I'm the man who slept in your little back room. You sure were kind to me and I haven't forgotten. I've been successful since I left you and I just came this morning to see if we could have a cup of coffee together."

Up the Ladder

As we sat there in front of that old fireplace in the warm glow of the crackling coals, he told me a story that I thought was true. He stated that he was now a chef in one of the finest clubs in Chicago, naming it; that he had bought a home for his mother and that he had saved forty dollars to bring me as a Christmas present. And with these words he took out a roll from his pocket. It looked so big that I know they were all one dollar bills. He put this in my lap. I have had a good many Christmas presents in my life, but that one pleased me the most of all. I was happy, though, to tell him that things were not as bad with me either, as they had been five years ago. "You see I have coal in the fireplace now," I said. Maybe he remembered that he brought in kindling for me before—kindling with resin on it—resin that made it look as if the fire were more than it really was; and that, after the two bundles were burned, I either went to bed or stayed up and shivered, because two bundles of kindling were the daily ration.

He reluctantly put back the money in his pocket. We said good-by. I wished him a merry, merry Christmas and the best of all New Years.

That evening I went to the home of a friend for dinner and I told of this proffered gift and of the gratitude in that poor man's soul. There was one rich guest there whose heart was deeply touched, and he said, "I am going to do something for that darky, if I never do another act in my life." He called up the club I had mentioned and was told that they never had had a colored chef during the existence of the club! So there I was; but, after all, he had been grateful. Oh, yes, there is a sequel.

Not many months later I was awakened in the middle of the night by the wild ringing of my bell; and as I had never been afraid at No. 42 East 31st Street—a main street, with a policeman always at the corner, and the street itself as light as day—I went to the door and opened it. There was my colored man, shivering with fear. "Fo' the love of God, missy," he chattered, "let me in!"

What else could I do but admit him? We closed the outside doors in the vestibule. I looked in his face. "What in the world is it now?" I asked. "Oh, let me sleep in the little back room just for to-night," he cried. Of course I did, but

THE LIVING ROOM ON 31ST STREET

My First Little Bond Shop

Up the Ladder

I expected the policeman to ring my bell. I did not close my eyes all night. At dawn I rapped on the back room door. But there was no answer. The poor old fellow had already crept away. I never heard of him again.

Another step-sweeper came not long after that, a strange-looking old man, who very timidly asked me if there was anything he could do. I told him about the little back room and Miss McGraw and the snow that had to be swept from the path in the back yard and the front steps. Also, I said, he could bring in the kindling and take out the ashes, if he wanted to. How grateful he too was, to feel that he was at last earning his own way. By this time all sorts of interesting people were coming to my house. Some were very rich and some were very poor. The rich ones wrapped their furs around them a little tighter when the fire grew dead, but we poor folks did not seem to mind the cold and I do not remember ever envying any of them a fur robe or luxurious woolens. My own fur coat was worn out. I think I was using the last of it for collar and cuffs on a coat I had made out of a blanket.

This special evening was Sunday and my old

helper came in with some kindling. But suddenly he was in a panic, turned, and rushed out. The next morning I asked him what in the world had been the matter the night before. "Mrs. Bond," he said, and he was shaking again, "one of your guests" (and he mentioned the name of a very well-known writer) "is my cousin. I don't suppose he'd recognize me; but I was so afraid. For many years he pulled me out of the gutter and tried to make a man of me; but I don't seem able to help myself. I am just a born drunkard. Yes, I've been sober since I've been in your house; maybe because I could not get anything to drink; but I think it's because I'm grateful; I'd hate to do anything to make you sorry. But I have to go. I'm past redemption. And one of these days I'd—well, I'd meet some one else I know, and they might know me."

A sad parting, for my heart ached for that poor man! He went; I could not persuade him to stay.

One lovely crisp Sunday morning, when I had done my housework and everything was in order—times were better, I had plenty to keep warm with, and all necessary things for com-

46

fort—I don't remember whether I had sold some china or silver, or whether I had had an òrder large enough to make things brighter, but anyway, everything looked brighter—by accident, there stepped into my apartment a gentleman who was to become one of my truest and most helpful friends.

Across the hall upstairs there was a little soubrette who had given up the stage and gone into an office to work. She had been, and was, a lovely singer. I scarcely knew her, but we had met in Miss McGraw's restaurant and Miss Mc-Graw had told me a good deal about her. She had come that morning to tell me she was off for an errand in the neighborhood, but was expecting two gentlemen to call. One was a manager and the other a singer. Would I take them in until she returned? They came. One was a fine-looking young man, who I thought must be the musician, the other, a very dignified man who fairly radiated success. I explained, and asked them to come in. Almost immediately, the younger man, whom I had taken to be the singer, went to the piano where there were three or four of my manuscripts on the rack, and even before he sat down, asked me if they were mine. I told him yes. "Would you mind playing these for me," he asked, and he began to sing.

The first song was "I Love You Truly." He was quite enthusiastic. He said he would like to sing it at once in public, if I cared to let him take the manuscript, or copy it.

Oh, how I longed to let him do that! But I did not have any copyright and was afraid to let any manuscript go out of my hands. But he promised me that as soon as this was properly taken care of he would be only too glad to sing my songs and to do anything he could to make them sell. He was Victor P. Sincere, a young lawyer. Music was his hobby. It was the beginning of one of the most valuable friendships of my life.

I would like to go back a little bit now, to another singer who was of great help to me. He happened to be in the office of Dunlap Smith and Company one morning when I went in to tell them that I could not pay my rent. This young man was standing in the office talking to his cousin, who was private secretary to Mr. Cobb. As I passed by and said good morning to her, she smiled, and I noticed there were tears in her eyes.

I supposed she was telling the young man some sad story, but I learned later that the tears she was shedding were for me, as she told her cousin how sorry she had been for me month after month, and that she thought I was brave, and all I needed was some help, if only she knew how to offer it. Then she told him my story, and he came to my house one day and introduced himself as George O'Connell. He had a beautiful tenor voice and from that day began to sing my songs. He has sung them ever since. Then he was studying in one of the big musical colleges in Chicago; he made every effort to make my songs better known.

These musicians were, of course, beginning to show me the way. I discovered that although I was giving recitals constantly in homes of friends for ten dollars an evening, it was a very slow way of advertising, and that I must meet public singers and get my music into their hands. It may have been Victor Sincere who suggested my going to call on Jessie Bartlett Davis, who years ago was the prima donna of the old Boston Opera Company, and who made "Oh Promise Me" famous the world over. And how she sang it in the opera,

"Robin Hood," for years! Well, one fine day, I telephoned to Jessie Bartlett Davis. We were too poor, of course, to have a telephone in the house; I went to the corner drug store, and, strange as it may seem, Jessie Bartlett Davis came to the telephone herself. I told her of my desire to meet her and asked her if she would listen to my songs. As I look back now, through my experience of all my years of going to the telephone and hearing some one say, "May I come up and sing some of my songs to you?" I think her kindness was most beautiful. Naturally, she was besieged by ambitious people—almost as much as I am to-day. I say almost as much as I am because, of course, her life was not along the lines that mine has followed. Hundreds of people who write songs seem to think that all that is necessary to make a song successful is to send it to me and have me pass judgment on it, or tell them just what to do with it—which has become an impossible thing for me to do, and, in many cases, would have always been an impossible thing to do. I have no idea but that thousands of songs, better than any I have ever written, have never been noticed; but no one in the world can tell why, any more than any one can be absolutely certain that the world is going to like a play. It is really one of the great gambling things of the world—the chances on what is going to sell.

Well, the hour came for me to call on Mrs. Davis. She did not keep me waiting. I went into her lovely music room and there she was to welcome me. "What can I do for you?" she asked. I told her as quickly as I could what I had done and how I had done it. I suppose her heart was touched by the looks of me. I was really ill and I do not know that I looked as though I were "homemade," but everything I had on I had made myself—hat, coat, dress—and as I had never been trained in the art of dressmaking or millinery, with the exception of that one day of which I spoke in another chapter, I very probably did look very homemade. If she noticed it she gave no hint, but I know I never looked *shabby*. I went to the piano and played the seven little songs which I had in manuscript, and which I so longed to have published. "You must have those published at once," Mrs. Davis said with fine enthusiasm, "and I am going to sing them!"

But the cost! It took a great deal of money to

print seven songs and make a book. That is what I wanted to do with these. I told her I had saved about two hundred and fifty dollars. The cost would be five hundred—the very lowest price. Without a word Mrs. Davis went to her desk, wrote something, came back and handed me a check. "Here is the extra two hundred and fifty dollars," she said. "Go get your other money; then go to your printer as quickly as you can."

Without giving me a chance to say anything she fairly pushed me out of the door. By the time I had gone half a block, I realized what had happened to me. Back to her house I rushed and told her how I appreciated her aid, and that I was going to accept it, but must give her a receipt because I always paid my debts and this one was going to be paid as quickly as possible.

She laughed and said, "Why, my dear, there is no need of anything like that between us. You know you have it, and I know you have it. And, besides, if you are very much worried about it, the check will receipt the bill. Forget it and get busy."

Well, I went on wings to Mr. Nelson's printing office. For the first time I paid him in advance. My little book of seven songs was launched. And this was all through the kindness of Jessie Bartlett Davis. Never did she cease to be my friend.

I had been told that a book of songs would never sell, especially one written by an unknown composer of music, but I could not bother with either doubts or fractions. I wanted something that would sell for a dollar and I made up my mind that this book would so have to be. This volume contained, "Parting," "Shadows," "Just a Wearyin' for You," "I Love You Truly," "De Las' Long Res'," "Still Unexprest," "Des' Hold My Hands." The two songs that made this book popular were "Just a Wearyin' for You" and "I Love You Truly." On account of their immense popularity they were finally taken out of the book and sold separately.

By this time I was my own publisher. As I said before, I had to have some sort of place in my little apartment to keep the music. Now in the upstairs part of the house where I lived was an extra room, in those days called "the little hall bedroom." I moved upstairs where the rent was twenty dollars, and in the closet off the hall bedroom I had some shelves put up. The depth of this closet was just the width of a sheet of music and that was my first stock room—the future Bond Shop. In it was a very small edition of the little book of seven songs—the seed of all my future business.

Of course, it is one thing to publish a book of songs and another to get it noticed; but I wondered why the stores did not care to stock my music. I did not know then that people did not buy things for which there was no demand, and I used to think those big stores were rather selfish. How much I had to learn! They were all just as kind as they could be. It was not possible for them to buy things they had no use for; and finally it dawned on me that nothing could be done until I created a demand for my music. I decided that I must find some way to advertise without money. I have often wondered if it would have been an easier path for me if I had been young and lovely? You know, I was thirty-four. Not only that, but sorrow had been well written on my face—my face that was always plain! So I really had to earn a place by the hardest efforts. I had nothing of particular interest to offer except my work.

Up the Ladder

When I went into a store and said, "May I show you some of my songs?" or "Will you listen?" when I tried to persuade them to let me play and sing in an office where there was a piano where they tried things out, they were always polite to me, yes, but I have always felt that had I been just a little more attractive I might have had just a little quicker attention. But, after all, patience is greater than beauty and I finally got a hearing in spite of everything.

Almost the first thing I did was to offer to sew in exchange for some free advertising in a musical magazine which was owned by a woman I knew. This helped, of course, but in a slow way; and the orders scarcely ever amounted to more than six or eight dollars a month. These orders I would deliver myself. Besides this, I tried to do the bookkeeping which was almost impossible for me. But always I kept up my little home.

At that time I was writing the words as well as the music for my songs, and also I painted the covers, as I had not money to spend on such things. For my title page I used a wreath of wild roses, and put a line underneath these flowers; in the center the legend, "Songs as Unpretentious as the Wild Rose." I did this because I was so afraid of criticism, and I thought those words would be my protector, and I really think they were. I never did pretend to be anything remarkable; I just had to write these songs as a matter of bread and butter. I think if I had been criticized, as I have read of some people being criticized, my heart would have broken. I do not think I could have stood anything more than those burdens I already bore. I remember only two unkind things that were ever printed about me—I mean that I ever saw. One was in a music magazine that, in later years, was very kind to me. It said, "Last night, at such and such a place, Carrie Jacobs-Bond sang some of her sob songs." Again, in a newspaper, after a concert which had meant the world to me, I read these words: "Carrie Jacobs-Bond is a plain, angular woman, writes plain, angular songs and sets them to plain, angular music." Later, when that newspaper woman was informed of the struggles of my life, and of the poverty I was passing through, she was sorry. She sent me word that she was sorry, but oh, that did not undo the hurt of it.

You see, I was actually forced into singing my own songs. But I do not think that people ever quite understood that my appearances in public were solely to advertise my songs. I never felt that I had any talent for the platform and I did such work each time in fear and trembling. Of course, I could always play fairly well, but up to this time I had never even spoken a piece in school, to say nothing of singing on the stage. I took very great care now to do my songs so they would be understood. That was all. And I was rewarded when Mrs. Mildred Adams, who was really a critic, told me one day that my work was artistic. She said she wished that her pupils had the diction I had, and for me to go on just as I was going, in my original way, and that I was bound to win. So I started, and so I persevered. For twenty-five years I gave these little recitals, coming up from ten dollars a recital to my last public performance, which was netting me a thousand dollars a week.

To begin with, these recitals were given in the drawing-rooms of my influential friends, who had evidently told my story to their friends, and for several years I went from home to home. I may have been poor in money but I have always been rich in friends.

In addition to the eleven songs which my first publisher had, I had written a book of four songs. One of the men in the first publishing house went into business for himself, and knowing that I had no agency or connection, had offered to publish this smaller collection, and he had been mighty nice about it. "Now, Mrs. Bond," he said, "any time you feel you would like to buy back these songs, I will let you have them for exactly what they cost me, because I know you are trying to establish a business of your own." As I had four songs lying idle, I let him have them. Sometime later I wanted the songs back, as it would help my own business to have more to offer the trade. I approached him and he agreed to let me have them for three hundred dollars, one hundred of which was to be paid down. Of course I didn't have the hundred dollars, but I thought I would try—much as I hated to borrow—to get this from some old friends. I therefore picked out three people, thinking that one, at least, might lend me the hundred dollars necessary to get immediate control of the book. Within a week, I had answers from all three friends, and each one had sent a hundred dollars.

These three hundred-dollar checks were rather appalling to me and I wondered if I were brave enough to keep them all. I finally said to myself, "Yes, you are," and I wrote a letter to each of these three friends explaining the situation exactly. Again, in reply, all three told me not to worry about it; to return the money when I could—and the best of luck!

One evening I was singing for a small group of people at the Art Institute in Chicago. After my short program a lovely auburn-haired lady, with the kindest eyes I ever saw, came to me. It was one of my ten-dollar concerts but it was the same concert for which I later was paid one hundred and fifty dollars an afternoon—the same old songs done in the same old-fashioned way. She of the kind eyes told me who she was—Mrs. Henry Howe, from Marshalltown, Iowa, and President of the Twentieth Century Club.

"I have heard quite a bit about you since I came to Chicago," she went on, "and I am very anxious to have you come to Marshalltown to give a recital for our club. Can you come? We will pay your expenses; and ah, yes, what do you charge for your recitals?"

I said, "Ten dollars." It seemed perfectly wonderful to me to be offered an engagement out of town with my expenses and ten dollars; and so that date was fixed.

In Marshalltown I went to the home of my friend. Happily, across the street, in that dear town that I grew to love so well, lived a distant cousin whom I had not seen since I was a child. I felt at home, and in every way this Marshalltown recital was a most happy occasion. It was thus, through Mrs. Howe, that my real recital work began. It was through many letters from her, and her great interest, that I sang in almost every important town in the State of Iowa.

It was while I was visiting at the home of Mr. Amos Steckle in Bloomfield, Iowa, in whose lovely music room I was to give a concert, that I was taken to hear Elbert Hubbard of East Aurora in a lecture on his shop and work. I had never known anything very intimate about the Roycroft Shop until I heard his talk; but I had read *The Philistine,* his magazine, in which he seemed to criticize every one, and I thought he was a **very**

unkind man until I met him. But oh, the interest
I took in that lecture, and the interest I took in
what he said about publishing your own things,
and what people said about people who did it, and
that you generally did it because you could not get
a publisher! In fact, he said that was what made
him start the Roycroft Shop; that he did not consider it a disgrace to publish yourself what you
wrote, or to advertise it; that if you did not believe it was good you would not want to publish
it; and if you believed it was good, why not publish it yourself? It would be rather a dishonest
thing to try to sell something you thought was
bad! I do not think I was ever more interested in
any one's talk in my life; and after it was over and
every one went back to speak to him, I went also.
"I had never been very much interested in you
before," I told him, impulsively, "but I must say
I think the Roycroft Shop is about the most wonderful place I ever heard of," and I started to tell
him something about myself.

He laughed and said: "Oh, I know all about
you, Mrs. Bond, through your friend, Grace Duffy
Boylan." He had mentioned one of my first newspaper friends, one whom I had met through my

blessed Amber. Incidentally, I may add, Miss Boylan, now Mrs. Louis Geldert, former National President of the League of American Penwomen, was always on the alert to further my interests by spreading the news of my little songs. Mr. Hubbard added, "In fact, I know two of your songs, 'I Love You Truly' and 'Just a Wearyin' for You,' and I think they are lovely. I would like to talk to you about them. Would you have time to see me in the next two days?"

He came to call. Almost his first words were, "Mrs. Bond, do you know just what you are looking for?" I answered, "Certainly; I am looking for a gate that leads from Chicago to New York where, I am told, the greatest opportunities for starting original things can be found. Yes, New York is where I want to go."

"Well," he said, "that is very easily arranged. If you care to come to the Roycroft Shop and give us a concert, I will give twenty-five dollars and your transportation to New York City and back, and you can stop at East Aurora."

Now, all I knew of East Aurora and the Roycroft Shop was what he had told me in his lecture; but it was a wonderful thing to me to think I might possibly see it all. And so the day came for me to leave.

I arrived at the little station in East Aurora to be met by the two Elbert Hubbards. Bert, the son, was then just a little boy, the age and size of my own son, and he was his father's partner, too. This was before the Roycroft Shop had great buildings of its own, but was built in the yard adjoining the Hubbard home and was called the "gymnasium." That was the only large room connected with the Roycroft Shops, and as I remember it was filled with great heavy tables packed with books ready to ship.

"This is where we are going to have the concert," they said. When evening came I went over from the house and found a real music hall awaiting me. The heavy tables had been pushed together to make a stage, and on the stage there was an upright piano, something I dreaded, as my work really required a grand piano. You see, I talked over the piano. But I played and sang the best I could with my back almost to the audience. They all said they enjoyed it, and such wholehearted applause I had never had. Of course Mr. Hubbard's speech before I began the recital would have made anything I did of interest to those dear people. He talked of me as if I were a great genius, and said that I honored them by coming— just as though I really were of great importance. Under these circumstances I did the very best I could. In those days my voice was full of tears, that I know; and it seemed to bring tears to the eyes of other people; and so, unless I had seen my audience affected as I was accustomed to seeing them in my small drawing-room work, I would have been disappointed, and would have felt that I was not doing my very best. But on this night I saw tears in the eyes of my friend, Elbert Hubbard, and I felt that possibly I was singing as well as I ever did.

In the first number of *The Philistine* printed after my recital was an article written by Mr. Hubbard—the first publicity of any importance I had ever received, and which, I felt, was the beginning of my being known to the world. It ran:

Art, at least, is a matter of heart, not head; and this fact was brought home to me strongly a few weeks ago on hearing Carrie Jacobs-Bond. Here is a woman who writes poems, sets them to music and sings them in a manner that reveals the very acme of art. Her performance is all so gentle, spontaneous and unaffected that you think you could do the same yourself—simple, pattering little child-songs, set to tunes that sing themselves. But in some way they search out the corners of your soul, and make you think of the robin that used to sing at sunset, calling to his lost mate, from the top of a tall poplar in the days of long ago. As a reader and singer, Carrie Jacobs-Bond is as subdued as a landscape by Cazin, and as true and effective as a sketch by DeMonvel.

I spent a week in this wonderful place, and while I was in the house of Elbert Hubbard, I made up my mind that in Chicago at No. 42 East 31st Street there was going to be a place called "The Bond Shop," and that it would begin in the hall bedroom, and all the inspiration would be credited to my good friend, Elbert Hubbard, who had done just this thing for many people before he met me, helping people to help themselves. That was always his greatest hobby. He was never interested in those who came to him expecting him to do their work so that they could succeed, but if he saw they were in dead earnest to help themselves, he would tell them how he thought they could best do it.

At the end of the week, Mr. Hubbard asked if I should like to go with them to New York City to the first Philistine dinner that had ever been planned. They were giving it for him, he said, and he was going to take Bert, and he would be happy to have me come along. What a mistake it would have been for me to have declined that wonderful invitation! That night at the Philistine dinner, which began at seven o'clock and lasted until three o'clock in the morning, I sat with Edwin Markham on my right and Bliss Carman on my left; and with a hundred other brilliant men and women I heard them laugh at Mr. Hubbard and say what seemed to me the most impudent things, while I thought him so fine and wonderful that I wanted to get up and tell every one how terrible they were to abuse him. Every one had said just what he wanted to say, and every one had laughed, except me, and, oh yes, Mr. Hubbard's face did not seem to change at all. He just looked on, in that wonderfully amused way that I learned afterward to understand. He really was having the time of his life and I did not know. Bert, little as he was, seemed to enjoy it more than any one else, for every little while he gave his father a sly glance.

Well, by and by, early in the morning, the toast-master said, "And now we will hear from Fra Elbertus," and we did!

He did not use any notes, but oh, how he did answer every jest! And I knew from that hour that he did not need any especial champion. He was perfectly able to take care of himself.

For twenty years after that, whenever I went to New York, I always went by way of East Aurora; and no matter what time of the day I arrived (I often went when I had only a few hours to stay) Mr. Hubbard would send word to the shops—which now were many and provided work for hundreds of people—"Carrie has come and she is going to sing for us." The shops closed and all the workers would come to the beautiful music room, which stood next door to where the gymnasium used to be, and I would give the concert.

No longer did we have to shove the tables together and lift the piano. There was a fine platform with a magnificent Mason and Hamlin grand piano on it, comfortable chairs, and beautiful surroundings, a frieze painted around the ceiling by a great artist.

Later, I gave here what was to be my most interesting program ever given anywhere. I had sent word long enough ahead this time to have the plans all made, and as it was in apple blossom time, Mr. Hubbard decided we would give a concert out-of-doors. So a platform was built around the great apple tree that stood in the center of the Roycroft yards, and the piano was brought outdoors. One lovely afternoon I sang with the apple blossoms falling down on the audience and on me—sang as hopefully and as freely as the birds sang, because it was an ideal place for music, and I was among true friends. You know, poverty does many things for you, but I feel that the greatest thing it does is to show you your friends, and I was so poor that I knew who mine were. I may have had some disappointments in life, but never through my friends. That is one of the advantages of being poor. Almost every one can have friends if he can give them something; but when you have nothing but yourself to give, and friends stand true—that means something.

The last visit was just four days before Mr. Hubbard started on that fateful journey which was to carry him to his death. I had come unexpectedly again, and once again the word was sent around, "Carrie has come and she is going to sing for us." I gave the program, and as usual, my stay was for just a few hours. I was hurrying away and was anxious to say good-by to him. He could not be found.

I asked Bert where in the world his father was, and he answered, "I am afraid he did not want to say good-by. He left the music room with tears in his eyes, and the last I saw of him he was on his horse going in the direction of the cabin. He called over his shoulder to me, 'Say good-by to Carrie.'"

The next time I went to East Aurora was to attend the funeral services for Mr. and Mrs. Elbert Hubbard, where hundreds of friends gathered to show their love and respect. We all stood with bowed heads and tears streaming down our cheeks beside the beautiful memorial stone which was placed in the garden of the Roycroft Shops to remind strangers of the man whose friends could never forget him—friends to whom no marker was needed to recall his many kindnesses.

A few months after this, a beautifully bound book was sent to me from the Roycroft Shop. It contained the original manuscript of a little story they found among his things, which he had written about me, evidently after my last recital at the Roycroft Shop:

Carrie Jacobs-Bond was along Roycroft way, and as usual when Carrie comes to East Aurora, she sang for us. We quit work and the boys and girls gathered in the music room and we listened. Carrie does not pretend to sing, and she knows she is not beautiful, but she certainly can play the piano, and Carrie Jacobs-Bond has personality. She is young, just my age, but time has tempered her, fate has buffeted her, destiny has dashed her dreams, but she has cashed in all her experiences so to-day you behold her—all her actions are regal, graceful, gracious, chartered with honesty, illumined by intelligence, flavored with success, and that is all success is good for, just to flavor; the thing in its pure state is nauseous. Carrie played and sang songs of her own, and one of those songs was "A Perfect Day"; and when I hear that song I think I hear the notes of a robin singing in the tree of my mother's dooryard, years and years ago. It must have been a perfect day when "A Perfect Day" was written, for the song has been more widely sold than any piece of music since Gilbert and Sullivan launched "Pinafore," and if you will agree not to mention it, "A Perfect Day" has passed its five million mark and has brought its composer thousands and thousands of dollars. Not so bad for a lone, lorn widow.

Going back to my first experience in New York City, where I had expected that great things would be much easier to find, I was greatly disappointed. I found that there was a wide demand for one who could write incidental music for theatrical performances of any kind; and also for songs to fit certain places in light operas. The incidental music I might have been able to undertake, but the other seemed quite too difficult.

However, some one told me that Della Fox was rehearsing for a new comic opera, and that she was very kind and probably would see me. I learned the name of the theater in which she was rehearsing and went there. I was ushered down toward the front of the auditorium. The first thing I saw through the dimness was the light of a cigarette. In a moment my eyes became accustomed to the dark, and I saw that the cigarette was being held by Miss Fox herself. In those days few women smoked. She was the first I had ever seen. It was rather a shock! I introduced myself in a very timid way and said I had been told she might possibly be interested in some of my songs for the play she was rehearsing. But my thoughts were: "She will never care for anything that I am writing," and she said, "Well, what kind of songs do you write?" "Oh, very simple homey ones," I said.

By this time I had found myself and recited a verse of a little song called "Where to Build Your Castles," never dreaming she would care the least about it. It was the first thing that came to my mind, that's all. But, to my surprise, she said, "Well, I never sing anything like that myself; but I have a lady in my company who could do it beautifully, and will ask her to sing it."

She did, and the song was put in the opera and was sung for a year. I am sorry I cannot remember the name of the opera, but it was very successful and this I do remember—Della Fox was perfectly charming.

Some one had convinced me, I have forgotten now who it was, that the best possible way for me to put my songs before the world was to sing them on the stage. There were very few chances of this kind at that time, because vaudeville was not in vogue. But there was, in Chicago, a gentleman named Middleton, who was one of the firm of Cole and Middleton. They had a museum; I think they called it a Dime Museum. He decided to start what is known now as vaudeville, in a theater, outside his other entertainment hall. He began his business down on State Street. It was not a very splendid place, and vaudeville thirty years ago did not amount to very much. But through his wife, he had become interested in my songs and offered to give me a hearing. My first appearance was to be on a Sunday afternoon. I had, at this time, a very devoted friend, an instructor of dramatic art, now Honorary President of the Federation of Music Clubs of New York, and very well known as Madame Marione. At that time she was busy teaching in Chicago. She was one of the people you call a friend in need. If I were ever in trouble I felt I could go to her; she had a wonderful way of encouraging you and showing you how you could help yourself, which, as I said before, is the only real help any one can give you—the only help that lasts. I told her of the opportunity and she said she thought it would be fine. So I finally told Mr. Middleton I should be more than grateful for the chance, and the date was set. About three weeks later, on a summer Sunday afternoon, I made my début.

I had never been on a stage in my life, and had not even been down for a rehearsal, as there was nothing to rehearse for. I knew the piano was there. I was to use an automatic player which was, at that time, a great novelty. I had made some records for this piano player, which had been invented and manufactured by George P. Bent of Chicago, another helpful friend. The performance which I was to give consisted of my sitting at this piano player, pumping it with my feet and manipulating some kind of push buttons, while the piano did the rest. Then I was to sing in my funny way some of my songs.

I arrived at the theater dressed in a little black

silk dress, which I had made myself; and to make it quite dressed up I had put in a white lace front and carried a bouquet of white lilies. For nine years I had dressed in mourning, and that white vest seemed to me to be almost too gay; but I felt I had to dress up some. I do not suppose any one can ever guess how odd I must have looked. At that time I did not know anything about stage presence, or appearances. All I knew was that I had on the best possible dress I could afford and I thought I had made it very gay by putting white on it. And hadn't I spent almost my last cent to buy the bouquet?

My dear friend, Mrs. Boylan, and my little son had gone up to the gallery to be sure to find out how my voice carried, and also to see how the people took me. Madame Marione went down to the dress circle.

As I came through the stage door I passed the first dressing room, where a little old-timer, a woman, called out to me cheerfully, "Who are you looking for, honey?" I said I was going to perform that afternoon—going to do an act, as one should say.

"What, looking like that?"

"Yes," I faltered.

"Come in here," she said good-naturedly, "and I will fix you up a little."

If there is any one in the world who thinks people behind the stage are selfish and unkind, I should like to tell them just a few of the wonderful stories I have learned by experiences I had in vaudeville, in later years, and from people on the stage in general. They may not be so kind after you have arrived, but then you do not need them so much; but when the struggler begins and these people see she is afraid and in need of help, I do not believe that one of them would fail to respond. No one could have been kinder than this dear soul who said she "would fix me up." Well, she did. When I looked at myself I was so well fixed I did not know it was I at all. Rouge, white paint, eyelashes and eyebrows!

"All this red on my face!" I gasped. "Won't I look terrible? And these awful red lips?"

"Scarcely noticed on the stage," she said. "That is the way you have to go."

So I went. In that audience there were just three people I knew were my friends. Well, the moment came for me to appear and I went to the piano player almost immediately. The gallery began to hiss, but I did not hear that. I knew there was some kind of commotion going on. The only words I heard were of cheer and comfort, such as "Don't let 'em scare you out, lady, keep a-goin'." This comfort from downstairs did not reassure me but I kept at it. I sang my songs and "pumped" my own accompaniment, and left the stage in full retreat! But I think I was the only person who knew that I had absolutely finished what I started out to do. Somehow I got through the dressing room and into the alley that led to the street, hatless and coatless. I ran down Michigan Avenue with pink tears dripping on my white vest, flying to my refuge, Madame Marione's rooms. I had forgotten that I had family and friends in the audience, until I found myself at the door. Then it dawned on me what I had really done. But I was not alone on Michigan Avenue. After me, as fast as his little legs could go, had come my boy; and throwing his arms around me, tears running down his cheeks, he said to me, as he always had, the encouraging thing, "Mother, it was just wonderful!"

Well, in a very few minutes my other friends came in and also Mr. Middleton, God bless him! He also told me it was splendid for my first time. "And now you come to-night," he added. "It won't be half as hard." I told him he'd have to excuse me—I knew I was not born for the stage. None the less my heart fluttered with gratitude and anxiety when I took a check from his hands and heard him saying he wished it was for a thousand dollars instead of twenty-five. I vowed then—oh, vanity!—that never again would I appear in public. It was simply one of those "nevers" that we sometimes vow because we cannot look ahead.

When I first began publishing my own songs I went to a fine printer by the name of Mr. Nelson, whose beautiful Sweden I saw for the first time only many years later. His printing plant was in two rooms on the fourth floor of a dilapidated old building on Dearborn Street, which was owned by Hetty Green. Mr. Nelson had the reputation of being the best printer of music in Chicago. An old-time craftsman, he knew his own shop thoroughly, and never let anything go out of his plant in which he did not take pride. He was a big, good-natured man, who, like so many of his race, was unemotional. In all the years I dealt with him he never sent me a bill nor asked me for a cent. He always took it for granted that if I had any money I would pay him. When I took him a song or group of songs to publish, I would always say, "Well, Mr. Nelson, I think I have a song now that is going to be a success," and in his quiet way he would answer, "I hope so." But my heart was always in my work so that I became weary of this apparent lack of enthusiasm, even though no man could have been kinder than Mr. Nelson was. One day I said to him, "Mr. Nelson, don't you ever dare to say 'I hope so' to me again. The next time I bring a song in and say I think it is going to be a success you must say to me, 'Of course it is, Mrs. Bond,' " and big as he was, I shook him. Of course he thought this was very funny, but he adopted the new formula all right. The changed words did not change the luck so far as I can recall.

All through my negotiations Mr. Nelson was the greatest help to me. It was he who recommended to me Mr. Henry Sawyer, a most competent musician and also a composer of no small talent, who took my music from dictation just as stenographers take down a letter, and almost as quickly. He had a great talent in his ability to catch by ear any music that he ever heard—that natural gift which was mine as well—and I would play a composition for him once and nearly always he would have it. I have heard remarkable stories about my inability to write my own music. I was not educated in composition, counterpoint, nor any of those technical things which would have helped me vastly, no doubt, in my compositions. But my music never had need of correction. No one has ever done any arranging, or has written any accompaniments for me. To begin with, I was able to make a manuscript that could have been used, although I admit it was often very poorly done, and very difficult for me to do. So, having Mr. Sawyer's help was a wonderful thing and we worked together for twelve years—in fact, always, until I came to California. Now, even if I had always done so and were capable of writing finished manuscripts of my songs, neuritis would have put an end to it. Nowadays it is difficult for me to write even so much as a letter. However, neuritis has never interfered in any way with my piano work, which is one of my greatest blessings, because it is at the piano that I do all of my composing.

Going back to Mr. Nelson: he helped me to keep my accounts and did all those things that were so difficult for me during those first seven years, because during that time there were no successes to speak of. It was the beginning. By the time success did begin to come, I had taken my boy into partnership. It was a business of which my son was the head, although Mr. Nelson never ceased to do my printing. Well, one day I asked Mr. Nelson how much I owed him. He went to his desk, took out a little book and said very quietly, "A little over fifteen hundred dollars." At those words I think my heart stopped. I had no idea I was in debt that deeply and I knew that Mr. Nelson himself was poor. There was very little profit in the kind of work he was doing for me. In fact, he was doing altogether too good work for the money he got from any one. I simply broke down with worry; and finally one day, I went to my old friend, Christine Forsythe. In her peaceful sanitarium

I had already spent many weeks. "This time," I told her, "I have come to die." I explained that I had no money, though I knew this never made any difference with her. "Put me in the cheapest room you have," I said. "I don't care where it is. And don't worry about me, because for the first time in my life I am discouraged and I tell you frankly, I have come to you to die."

She put me in a dear, quiet, little room and sat by me for hours. We both were too heart-broken to speak. She had counted on me and believed in me for seven years. Many times she had tried her very best to have me give up and come to her and stay until I was well, but that seemed an impossible thing to do. So, as we sat there, I finally told her just what I wanted her to do, and what to tell my son.

"Haven't you some old friend," she asked me at last, "some one you have known longer than you have me, some man who would know more about business than I could possibly know, and who could help your son carry on?"

For a long time I thought and finally said, "You know, Miss Forsythe, I have not let any of my old friends know where I live. None of

them knows a thing about this struggle of mine.
I don't think I could have borne their sympathy.
I've seen but one old friend in years and she
found me by chance one day just at noon. I felt
I must offer her something for luncheon, but in
my pantry there was nothing but tea and crackers
and I shared these with her, but without an explanation. I never knew what she thought, but
neither did I speak one word about my poverty.
That experience was enough. It made me feel
more than ever that I never did care to see any
one from home."

Yet my mind ran back. There was a certain
dear old friend, I remembered, in Janesville,
where our gardens had joined. We had played
together from the time we were three years old
until she married and went to Chicago to live.
Her husband was Mr. Walter H. Gale, later
one of the partners of the Gale and Blocki Drug
Company, a man of means and position. I had
never seen either of them since Dr. Bond's death;
they knew nothing of my adversities or where I
lived. But through Miss Forsythe's persistence
I sent for Mr. Gale. He came to the sanitarium
at once and I told him my story—that I was in

debt, that I was sick and knew I was going to die, but still had faith in my songs and must have something from them as an inheritance for my son. I had done all I could; the path was too rough for me to walk any longer; that was all. And since I had to tell some one, Miss Forsythe had advised me to tell him. Dear Walter Gale asked how I had fallen into debt like that and I told him through the printing of my songs; that I owed Mr. Nelson fifteen hundred dollars.

He said, "Well, you must have been selling some songs to have a bill as large as fifteen hundred dollars for printing."

"Oh, yes, we were selling songs, but something must be the matter, and I wasn't a business woman."

"No," he said, "there is nothing the matter; you have merely started a business without any money and I think you are quite wonderful to have done it. You always have to borrow money if you have none and are going to start a business. In fact, you are about the only person I know of who ever started a business with no money and arrived, as you have."

He did a little figuring and said, "I will lend you the fifteen hundred dollars."

I thought I could not borrow any more. I felt I was all through with borrowing, but when I looked up into his encouraging face I had another thought. "Just how much do you think my business worth?" I asked.

"Well, as I figure it out," he replied, "I should say it is worth about nine thousand dollars."

I remember I instantly sat up in bed and exclaimed, "What!" And a feeling, such as I had never experienced before or since, came over me. "Do you believe this?" I cried. "Do you believe it enough to buy a tenth interest in it?"

He quietly went to the little desk, wrote out a check for fifteen hundred dollars, handed it to me and asked, "When can Cora and I come to see you?"

This reunited friendship of so many years was wonderful for me, for we began again where we had left off in childhood; and from that day on to the death of these two beloved friends of mine, we were like brother and sisters. He was my silent partner and Cora was one of my most precious companions.

The next morning I left the sanitarium. In a few days I was able to go down town. I took that fifteen hundred dollars to my astonished Mr. Nelson. Then came the Bond Shop, with "Carrie Jacobs-Bond and Son, Inc."

Incidentally, that first year Mr. Gale made ninety per cent on his investment. But, you see, he never expected that. He was a druggist and did not know anything at all about music publishing. He was more surprised than any of us when he found what had really been accomplished. Of course, after this, "A Perfect Day" was written, and he came in for his share.

About ten years after that, Mr. Gale was sitting in our office—we now had beautiful offices on Michigan Avenue, with a real sign on the boulevard and seventeen people working for us sending out songs, perhaps as many as four hundred thousand sheets a month—and he laughingly said, "Would you like to sell another tenth interest in the Bond Shop?" I told him I would. "What will you take?" I asked him what he would give. "Would you consider eighty-five hundred dollars?" he said. I asked him if he were in earnest. He nodded his head and wrote me a check for the amount. As he handed it to me, he asked, "Do you know what you are going to do with it?" I answered, "Yes, buy a home and go around the world"—something I had hoped to do for a good many years.

And that is what I did. I bought a little house in Hollywood, then a beautiful little suburb of Los Angeles which at that time probably did not have more than fifteen hundred people in it; and I took the longed-for, hoped-for, journey around the world.

When I first began work in Chicago, of course, I tried to make friends among the music publishers and the piano people, and I was successful in so far as it was possible for them to help an unknown composer.

Among the first of these new friends I made was Mr. Carl Bronson, then with the Cable Piano Company. He and Mrs. Bronson became interested in my work, and through his influence with that company they decided to help me and offered to give a testimonial concert if I could provide the artists. This was a most wonderful offer of help. They furnished Steinway Hall, a beautiful

Mason and Hamlin piano, all the printing of window cards and programs of announcement and invitations. But how well I remember distributing those window cards, all I could possibly carry in a music case, going from store to store, asking them if they would please put the cards in their windows—and every one was kind. I was never embarrassed one moment of all those days of travel up and down the business streets of Chicago.

But before this was done, I went again to my dear friend, Jessie Bartlett Davis, and with great hesitancy asked her if she would consider singing some of my songs in a testimonial concert that was to be mine if I could produce the singers. How sweetly she said, "Yes," and helped me to think of others to ask. Among these was the late Charles W. Clark, who was at that time Chicago's greatest baritone; Paul Schloessing, cellist from the Thomas Orchestra; and a little girl who lived in my neighborhood, whom I had taught to sing my children's songs. All offered to come gladly and sing for me.

Through my friend, Victor P. Sincere, I had met Governor and Mrs. Richard Yates, of Spring-

Testimonial Concert and Reception

Tendered the Popular Author-Composer, CARRIE JACOBS-BOND, at

Steinway Hall, Friday Ev'g, February 28th, at 8:15 P. M.

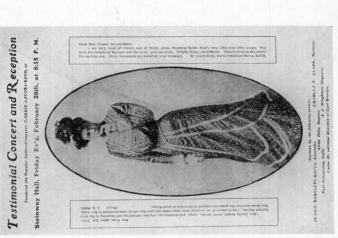

DEAR MRS. CARRIE JACOBS-BOND :

I am very fond of violets and of fresh, clean, morning fields—that's why I like your little songs. You have the insight of the seer and the poet—you see deep. Simple things are difficult. There's work in the world for such as you. Many thousands are awaiting your message. By yours truly, DAVID FRANGKON-DAVIS, Berlin.

"Mrs. Carrie Bond's short stories, songs and sketches are original, refreshing and inspiring to the very highest degree. I never enjoyed an evening more than when she gave her whole entertainment in New York. Mrs. Bond deserves the generous support of all lovers of good things."

New Tork, April 2nd 1901.   J. K. PAUL.

JESSIE BARTLETT-DAVIS, Contralto.   CHARLES W. CLARK, Baritone.
Little Olive Haynes,   Wrightson, Organist.
Paul Schoessling, Cello.
Under the personal direction of Carl Bronson.

PROGRAM

CONSISTING ENTIRELY OF MRS. BOND'S COMPOSITIONS.

PART FIRST.

Organ Prelude.   Mr. A. J. Wrightson.

Monologue—(Characteristique).
    "Talkin' Bout Little Things."

Songs of Child Life.
    a—"Shadows."
    b—"When God Puts Out the Lights."
    c—"I'm All Lady."
    d—"His Buttons are Marked U. S."
    Mrs. Carrie Jacobs-Bond.

Solo.
    "Ave Weakness."
    Jessie Bartlett Davis.

Cello Solo.   "Trigani Dances"
    Mr. Paul Schoessling.

Baritone Solos—Selected Songs.
    a—"The Stranger in Three Eyes."
    b—"The Lily and the Rose."
    c—"I Love You Truly."
    d—"When There's a Kernel."
    e—"God's Gay Day." (written expressly for Mr. Clark.)
    Mr. Charles W. Clark.

PART SECOND.

Characteristique—"Chimney Swallows."

Songs.
    a—Soul Unexpressed."
    b—"When I Am Dead, My Dearest." (Vocal.)
    c—"A Little Lullaby—sung a—
    d—"In The Chapel of The Broomcock Cavalry."
    Mrs. Carrie Jacobs-Bond.

Songs of Childhood.
    a—"Have You Seen My Kitten?"
    b—"My Boy's Going Home"
    Olive Haynes.

Songs.
    a—Selections from book of "Eleven Songs."
    b—"Love's Sacred Trust." (written expressly for
        Jessie Bartlett Davis   Mrs. Davis)
    a—"That Much Boy and His Mother."
    b—"My Old Man's Heaven."
    c—"The Woodman's Story."

Monologue—(Characteristique).
    Some Little Songs of Color.   Monologue—"Loyal"
    Mrs. Carrie Jacobs-Bond.

Organ Solo.   "Postlude"
    Mr. A. J. Wrightson.

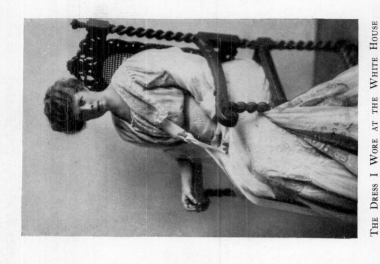

The Front of This Dress Is All That Was
Left of the Lace Curtain Dress

The Dress I Wore at the White House

field, Illinois, who also had been more than kind to me, and for whom I had given two concerts at the mansion, and who, in later years, were of the greatest help—something of which I will speak further on. I wrote to them asking them if they would allow me to use their names on my list of patrons, and they did not wait to write a letter— they telegraphed me. Yes, indeed, they would come up to Chicago for the concert and bring one hundred friends! Which they did. To any one who knows Chicago, this list of patrons will mean something; but after all, that means very little in comparison with their friendship.

Then came the great problem of what to wear. Any woman in the public eye, especially on the stage, knows that what to wear sometimes means success or failure; and the plainer you are, the more stylish you have to look because you have to make your audience forget certain things, and sometimes a stylish dress and the way you wear it does the trick. Well, what to wear? How I blessed my stars I knew how to sew and make a dress! But what to make it out of with no money was a problem. Once again my lucky star was shining and I went to the dear old box that had held some treasures of a former time, and there I found two beautiful lace curtains that had hung in my home, and two yards of white satin, grown a little yellow with time, it is true, but an unused piece just the same.

Well, I cut that two yards into little narrow strips about two inches wide, and cut the dress out of the lace curtains, and applied those satin strips by using a feather stitch and French knot embroidery. I know I did thousands of yards of feather stitching on that dress; every spare moment for four weeks I worked, and just an hour before time to go to the concert I put on the last French knot.

With me on this eventful night was my friend Madame Marione. As ever, she was by my side at all great moments. By the time I was dressed in my lace curtain and satin I began to realize the dreadful thing I was about to do—my second appearance on the stage! But I felt that this could not be quite as terrible as the first one, because I now had many friends in the audience, and at least I felt sure there would be no hissing or booing; I could look into the faces of people who knew me and who were there to help.

It was a bitter cold night, and a long drive from 31st Street to Steinway Hall. We rode in an old barouche, drawn by two weary old horses, weary as I was. My son sat on one side and my dear friend on the other, chafing my trembling hands. All I can remember from then on was saying, "I shall die before I get there"; and in after years my friend Madame Marione said she would not have been surprised if I had died, as I had used up every last bit of my strength.

But just as people do things under great pressure, so did I. I walked into the dressing room with frightened confidence, and there was my friend, Jessie Bartlett Davis, wearing the loveliest Paris dress I had ever seen. Twenty years ago hand-embroidered dresses were not so common as they are to-day, and her dress was white satin embroidered with great clusters of purple grapes and green leaves. As I looked at her she said, "Yes, this is a new dress bought just for this concert. I know by your face you like it." But she hurried on to say, "And what a lovely dress you have on! Where did you get it?" The best of it was that I knew she meant every word she said. I certainly was happy when

I could tell her I made it myself. "I hardly believe it," she cried, but she said she guessed she would have to, because she knew well enough I did not have money to buy one.

Apparently the concert was a great success. I had to my credit about seven hundred dollars, thanks, be it said, to Mr. Bronson and the Cable Piano Company. All the morning papers were kind in their criticisms; of course, very enthusiastic about the great artists who had assisted me. One critic said she could not understand why such an auspicious occasion should be given to Carrie Jacobs-Bond and that it really should have been given to Jessie Bartlett Davis, and then those words which hurt my feelings so much—that I was "a plain angular woman who wrote plain, angular songs, and set them to plain, angular tunes."

When this article came to the notice of Jessie Bartlett Davis she sent for that newspaper woman and explained to her how very poor I was and that I knew even then what it was to be cold and hungry; that I had made my own dress because I was too poor to buy one; that I was still making every sacrifice in order to gain recogni-

tion for my music. She told her I had never re-
garded myself as a singer, only as a writer of
simple little songs that I hoped would touch the
heart. The reporter said she deeply regretted
her words, and would like to meet me and tell
me so. But that meeting never came. I had
been too deeply hurt.

These lines of Will Carlton come to my mind
when I think, in spite of myself, of the few things
that were ever said that almost crushed me:

Boys flying kites haul in their white-winged birds,
But you can't do that way when you're flying
words.
Thoughts unexpressed can sometimes fall back
dead,
But God Himself can't help them when they're
said.

For at least ten years after I read that article
I never appeared in public without wondering if
my audience was thinking of me as plain and
angular; and it was ten years also before I felt
the least particle of comfort on the stage on account of those words.

CHAPTER III

SUNNY SLOPES

THE space allotted these stories is all too short to tell half that I would of the wonderful friends that were mine during the struggles of these years; but among them was dear Mrs. Bessie Gardner of Chicago, whose interest I won through her hearing some of my little songs, and she invited me to her home to give recitals. Finally, one day she said, "I have written to my friend Mrs. Frank J. Mackay who lives in London and who is entertaining in a very splendid manner. I have told her of your songs and have received a letter saying she would be delighted to have you come to London. She will pay all of your expenses and give you a hundred dollars." Can you imagine what that sounded like to me? At first I said, "I cannot possibly go!" "Oh yes, you can," Mrs. Gardner assured me. "You cannot afford not to go; it is a great opportunity and you are going to be paid for it."

Things were a little better now, but not quite affluent enough to buy many fine clothes. A few months before this opportunity came I had met some English people who were visiting in America. The husband was a singer and teacher and lived in London. I was only too glad to introduce him to my musical world and he seemed very grateful. Long before I ever dreamed of going to London, he said, "If you ever come to England come to us; we will be very happy to take care of you in our home." Hence with this invitation from Mrs. Mackay, and the remembrance of the other invitation, I thought I would not be entirely among strangers, so I wrote to my English friends, asking if I might come to their home, and received a very cordial answer.

I started for England—my first great professional journey—and arrived at the home of my friends; but I discovered immediately upon telling them of my mission that I had antagonized the singer, who, thoughtlessly, no doubt, exclaimed, "My, what an opportunity for an unknown musician! I have lived in London for years, and have given my life to training my voice, but no such thing has ever happened to me."

From that moment I felt I was not a welcome visitor, and wondered what I was going to do. I left the house, presumably for a little walk, but I went down to the very heart of London, and was wandering along Piccadilly when I found to my horror that I was fainting. A kindly-disposed policeman came by. "Are you ill, madam?" he asked. I answered that perhaps I was, I felt so faint. Then I remembered that I must have been walking for hours and had nothing to eat since breakfast. "Mr. Policeman," I said, "I must be feeling like this just because I have forgotten to eat my luncheon. Is there a place near here where you can take me?" "Right in here," he replied. We walked a few steps, the policeman helping me, and went into a restaurant. I looked around to see where I should sit, when lo and behold, who should be facing me but my friend in need—my dear Madame Marione with all her family! You can imagine what it meant at such a moment to see my friend who had always been with me in my greatest troubles, standing before me, with her hands outstretched!

Even the policeman looked as if he wanted to cry. We were so happy, the tears were streaming down our cheeks. "How in the world," I cried, "did this happen?" "Why," she explained, "we came over unexpectedly and did not know your address. Just our luck that we met!" As usual, I told her my trouble. "Of course you cannot stay in that house feeling as you do," she comforted me. "Probably he did not mean it as it seemed to you, but I think you should have a little place where you can be alone. It will be for only a few days. I will leave the others and go with you now; we'll find a spot."

We had a nice, warm luncheon, I sitting there with my dear friends and feeling that all the world was fine. We left the café on Piccadilly and went to a place my friend knew about on Russell Square. There we found a good boarding house, where, for ten dollars a week, I could have a room up four flights of stairs, with no fire. It was in the spring, but I remember it was very cold. My friend saw me settled, left her address, and telling me to call upon her any time, said good-by.

This boarding house was run by a blessed

woman named Emily Paine, who had lived in London all her life and had kept this particular boarding house for forty years. The only place she could tell me where she had ever been for any recreation was around the corner to the British Museum. When I asked her how long it would take us to go to Windsor Castle, she said she did not know exactly, but would find out. "Haven't you ever been there?" I asked her. "No, never," and she never had expected to go. I told her that I did, and would take her with me. This is a little out of the story, but we went, and spent one of the happiest of days. Mrs. Paine called it her red-letter day, and I guess it was mine also.

Well, the next day I was to meet Mrs. Mackay at Grosvenor Square, where she lived in a grand mansion that belonged to a Russian prince. Mrs. Frank J. Mackay was one of the most popular American women in the royal set at that time. She was very, very handsome, and as kind as she was beautiful. After we had luncheon in the most elegant style, she took me to the music room and asked me to sing for her the songs I had planned for my program. I was expected to sing four songs, two in each group. When we reached the music room, almost her first words were, "Caruso is to sing on this program, too." I was terrified! To sing on the same program with Caruso! His name, of course, was familiar to me, although he was not yet known in America to any great extent. Besides Caruso there was to be a young lady (her name I do not recall), to play the violin.

I played and sang the little songs I had sung at home with success; but when I finished, Mrs. Mackay sighed and said, "Oh dear, Mrs. Bond, those songs will never do; they are too sad; no one wants to cry; haven't you something brighter to sing?" Like a flash I thought: "I wonder if I have to sing those children's songs I so dislike to sing, but which every one wants to hear?" And I timidly said, "Yes, I have some children's songs," and I sang four of them for her. "Those will do beautifully," she was good enough to say. The only one I can remember was "I Am the Captain of the Broomstick Cavalry."

The night of the concert came. I wore a little white lace dress, the material for which had been given me by my friend Mrs. Gardner, but which I myself had made. The lace was really beautiful and I did not feel as homemade as usual, for some reason or other. Maybe I was too frightened at this time to think anything about what I wore. I arrived early, and as I entered the great hall I saw a picture I shall never forget —shimmering lights, garlands of natural flowers festooned around the ceiling and balustrade.

I walked up the magnificent white marble stairs and looked into the music room which was also a bower of beauty. Here, too, there were festoons of flowers around the ceiling. Great rose trees in bloom had been arranged so that their sprays ran over the doors and windows. At the end of this room was a stage banked solid for about three feet from the floor with pink, white, and blue hydrangea blossoms; a beautiful gilt piano was in the center of the stage. In the middle of the room, placed about four feet apart, were exquisitely carved and gilded chairs. I wondered why they were placed so far apart; but later, when I looked at the audience, I discovered that it was in order that the magnificent trains of the lovely ladies might be spread out properly, to show their beauty.

Until then I had never seen and have never seen since, such a wonderful sight. Lights from great crystal chandeliers made the jewels shine like stars in fairyland. Mrs. Mackay was magnificent in white satin, with three ostrich feathers in her hair, and the most gorgeous diamonds I had ever seen. This was the gown in which she had been presented to King Edward and Queen Alexandria.

I was taken into the little green room at the side of the stage. Very soon Caruso came in with a genial, happy smile and a "good evening" which was all the English I heard him speak. But there was nothing to be afraid of, or even anxious about, in the presence of that man. He was all kindness.

I do not recall much of the program; I was too frightened. But first came the violinist; then my two little songs; then Caruso. This was repeated and then it was time to go home. We were served wine and little cakes in a room by ourselves. No one had spoken to us, and we were ushered out. But as I reached the door a gentleman hurried down the stairs and said, "Mrs. Bond, it was delightful. I love your little 'Captain' song." This was the late Joseph Choate, then our Ambassador to the Court of St. James, and I shall never cease to be grateful to him, for, aside from his words, the evening had been—well —a most terrible experience. Not only did I feel that I had been a failure, but oh, I felt so alone! I got into a little one-horse shay and for fifty cents was driven home to Russell Square, where I climbed the four flights of stairs to my cold little room.

The next day I was invited to a party at the home of Sir Johnston Forbes-Robertson, one of England's leading actors. He and his lovely wife, Gertrude Elliott, made me very happy. I had met them a few days before the concert, and explained to them my mission in London, so they were anxious to know something about it.

Among the guests at this party was Sir (then Mr.) Arthur Wing Pinero, the great playwright and critic, who said to me: "I hear you appeared at Mrs. Mackay's concert last night; were you a success?" "No, indeed, Mr. Pinero," I replied, "it was a dreadful failure." "I am very sorry," he said; "of course I know it would be a difficult place to appear. But did they talk while you sang?" "Oh, no; they didn't do that." "Well, did they applaud afterward?" "Yes, they applauded." "Ye gods," he shouted. "You are a success. If they had not liked you they would not have applauded at all, and they would have talked."

I tried to be comforted because I knew that the author of "Mrs. Tanqueray," "Mid-Channel," and so many other famous plays, knew what he was talking about.

A few days later, I was invited to sing my little songs at a duchess's garden party, but even had I possessed the proper clothes to wear I could not have gone—not even for all the prestige and money I might have received. That first concert had been too terrifying. Of course my heart was heavy with the thought that my friends at home, who had been so kind in getting this wonderful engagement for me, might feel that I had neglected an opportunity; but not even to overcome this feeling could I go. I had been much more, unspeakably more, uncomfortable than that first afternoon at Mr. Middleton's theater on State Street in Chicago. Yet, what a difference!

Sometimes people who are too rich and too comfortable forget what tenderness means, and it was harder to forgive that gorgeous audience than it would have been that crowd of the poor who had suffered disappointment in State Street, having spent its hard-earned money and feeling it had got nothing in return.

Before I left London I had met some lovely, and also important people. I was invited to the home of Sir Annon Bryce, brother of the famous Ambassador to America, Sir James Bryce, and here I met a wonderful group of people, the sort I was accustomed to, people who were doing things. That evening stands out particularly as one of my happiest in London. In a few days more I started for home.

Apropos of old-time friends, however, I think perhaps one of the greatest helps that was given to me in those early years came through Governor Richard Yates, when he appointed me as one of the Child Labor Inspectors in Chicago—a position I held for six months, and for which I was paid eighty-five dollars a month—the most money I had ever earned up to that time. Of course this money was a wonderful help, but the experience was even greater. There is nothing in the world so touching to me as an unhappy little child, or the thought that in a great city like Chicago, and, for that matter, in every other great city, little children are put to work by ignorant parents when an education is waiting for them, free. In Chicago, even in those days, any child could go to the public schools; the women's clubs of Chicago had even promised to pay the family to whom these children belonged the same amount of money they could have earned. Yet, in spite of all, we often had to go to homes with a policeman to compel some parents to send their children to school. So it was among the very poorest, the most ignorant class of people, that I worked those six months. Up and down back stairs, in cellars, in garrets, dark and cold, we went. Sometimes we found little children working whose parents had lied about their ages so they could have the money these poor little creatures earned. That was another state of life I had known nothing about before I came to Chicago. I had never heard of such a thing. The situation I think is better now, after thirty years, but it finally crushed me. The haunting faces of sad little children was harder to bear than the loss of money, and I gave it up.

One of the most uncomfortable things that ever befell me, but which really appeared comical after a while, was the occasion of something written about me in California. I had been singing in Long Beach, and just as I was leaving the dressing room for the stage, a rip appeared in my homemade dress. I asked a friend who was with me to pin it. Just as I stepped on the stage the pin emerged a bit and stood on its point sticking straight into my shoulder. As I went to the piano I tried my best, by squirming, to make myself a little more comfortable. The pin did not move. I had to keep on with my numbers until the finish—and I did. The next day one of the critics said that my songs were very enjoyable and my rendition of them unique, but that I had some peculiar and unfortunate mannerisms which would probably wear off as I became more experienced in concert work.

As a matter of fact, I never have liked appearing before the public, and I always looked forward to the time when my work should become well enough known so that I need never do it again; but once you enter the field in which your work takes you, it is not so easy to escape, and people seemed to like my little songs in the way that I did them.

How well I can remember at this time hearing such things as, "Oh, yes, she does her own songs because you see she cannot get any one else to do them!" In a way, that was true; but I had not tried very hard. I did not know how. One thing, though, I firmly resolved, and that was never to hire any one to sing my songs. If they did not sing them because they really wanted to, I felt it would never be worth while to have them done at all, and no singer has ever asked me for pay.

I did present my songs to musicians, naturally, but I had my own way of doing it. I never sent very many songs to prominent singers—too many people do that—but to those only whom I felt would be in sympathy with my style of writing; and to those whom I felt I should not be afraid to meet, I used to send my songs, with a letter asking them please to look them over. How foolish it is for any one to insist upon a hearing of his work! When the person with whom you are talking is not very interested, instead of working in your favor, it makes for an even greater lack of interest. Of course there is a certain persistency which must be followed; but compelling or trying to compel some one to give you his precious time works a great deal of harm. One must also remember that singers are overwhelmed with songs constantly; even were they so inclined, they could not possibly look after all the manuscripts that are sent to them.

Very early in my career, Madame Nordica came to Chicago to appear in opera. Some one suggested that I send her one or two songs, but I first wrote and asked her if I might do so. In reply came a cordial note naming an hour. She was traveling in her private car, which had been sidetracked near the lake front in Chicago. The day was a stormy one of snow, sleet and rain, I had great difficulty in finding the car, and I presume Madame Nordica was surprised to have me call on such a day at all, but she invited me in and gave me an hour of her undivided attention. After looking over my songs she even promised, when she returned from concert work, that she would sing one of them. Shortly afterward she went abroad—and died; but I have never forgotten her gracious presence. She was one of the most beautiful women I have ever seen, and I still treasure the autographed picture which she gave me that day.

Later, I sent my songs to Madame Schumann-Heink, but when I did not hear from her, I let the matter drop, as I did not wish to prejudice so brilliant a singer against my modest work. But later, when I was singing at a convention in Atlantic City, I was invited to go to hear Schumann-Heink sing and went with friends to meet her. When she heard my name she immediately said, "I have some of your songs, Mrs. Bond; but I have not yet been able to look them over. I will some day." "I have been writing a song that I wish to dedicate to you," I told her, "if you would permit me. May I come to see you to-morrow?" "I am leaving to-night for my country place, Singac, New Jersey," she replied, "but if you can plan to come there to see me any time this week, I will be happy to go over your song with you, and perhaps I can use it."

This was one of the happiest occasions. Two days later I left for New York and on to Singac. Schumann-Heink's car was waiting for me at the station, and I was driven immediately to her charming home. We went into a great music room where the piano was in the center of the floor. The only thing I really remember about this room was a great white bear rug; there was very little furniture. At a glance it seemed to me an ideal place to sing, but no one can understand what an ordeal it was for me with my lack of skill to sing for one of the world's greatest singers. She was so kind that I finally found it possible to go on. So I sat down at the piano and sang "His Lullaby" (words by Robert Healy).

You cried in your sleep for your mother, dear
  Ba-by, Ba-by,
I would you could call her back to us here,
  Ba-by, Ba-by.
The little lambs are asleep on the sod,
And my own lamb-kin's beginning to nod,
And over the starlight your mother's with God,
  Ba-by, Ba-by.

Sunny Slopes

Sleep has come to the birds with the dew,
* Ba-by, Ba-by,*
Her eyes were as blue as the eyes of you,
* Ba-by, Ba-by,*
Dreams for your slumbers come up from the deep,
I'll love as she loved till morning lights peep,
And mother above us will watch while we sleep,
* Ba-by, Ba-by.*

I did my very best, and when I finished, she was weeping. "I'm going to do that very thing to my audience," she said; "just what you have done to me! I am going to sing that little song right away, and people are going to cry when I sing it."

They did, and I joined the audience with many a tear. She sang this "Lullaby" for many years, and sang also the only song I ever wrote that had anything to do with war—the song "My Son."

My son! I proudly see him marching by,
My only son who goes, maybe, to die.
The smile he sends me, as he hurries past,
Will cheer my soul as long as life shall last.
* My son! My son!*

The Roads of Melody

My son! Along the battlefield he goes,
The agony of love a mother knows,
Is following him through every hour each day,
To be his comfort on his lonely way,
My son! My son!

Again my son is proudly marching by;
In all this world there's only he and I;
Thank God! Thank God! The victory's won;
The world has freedom and I have my son.

Having mentioned the war, may I digress a
moment?

One night I was singing at a benefit for the
soldiers in a tent on a beautiful lawn in some
one's garden in Hollywood. As I stepped on the
stage, a dear little puppy came up to me, and
I picked him up and patted him. The gentleman
who had been introducing me had been auctioning
things off all evening, and he immediately said:
"Here is a perfectly good puppy that Mrs. Bond
has admired. I am going to sell him; what am
I offered?" No one said another word for quite
a while; the silence became embarrassing. Then
a voice from the rear of the audience said,
"Thirty-five." We did not hear anything else.

Naturally, thinking it was thirty-five dollars, the gentleman began to urge others to bid. "Thirty-five dollars," he cried. "I am offered thirty-five dollars! Who will give me thirty-six?"

But the time was limited and he had to say, "Sold for thirty-five dollars! Will the bidder kindly step forward?" Down the aisle with bowed head walked a dear old man in ragged clothes. He whispered to the auctioneer and this gentleman handed him the little dog. He started around the side of the tent, and as I looked at him I saw tears falling on the puppy's head. The auctioneer said, "Say folks, you never heard anything quite as sad as the story I am going to tell you." He went on: "That old gentleman handed me thirty-five cents and whispered to me, 'I got word to-day that my boy was killed at the front. I am sorry I did not understand you, but thirty-five cents is all I have.'"

Immediately I said to the audience, "Oh, give me some money, give me some money for that poor old man!" I do not think it was one minute before I had a friend's hat filled with money. I rushed off the stage and around to the back of the tent in time to find the old man caressing the poor little dog and sobbing as though his heart would break. I put the money in his pockets. I never knew how much it was, but I am sure it was a hundred dollars at least; and from that time on the evening was wonderful. Everybody spent money as I had never seen them spend it before.

That is the way with the world—if it finds some one really in need, those who have the money are willing to give. But people do get tired sometimes of giving because so often what they give is misused. That night, in the Hollywood garden, they probably would have done a great deal, as they did all through the war; but to be brought in close touch with the agonizing sorrow of that old man—that went to everybody's heart.

* * *

I must write a word for Chicago, dear Chicago, where for seven years I fought with poverty and became acquainted with what life means in a great city. But when Chicago realized that I was fighting for self-support and against great odds she opened her heart to me and the people helped all they were allowed to. You see I wanted to fight my own battle but the best general needs help and I found it in the hearts of the Chicago people.

My good friends were always ready to find opportunities for me to meet professionals. Often they were not people who could help me directly, but only indirectly through their influence and interest. One day, Madame Paul Picard, whose husband had been a schoolmate of Madame Bernhardt, asked me if I would like to meet that great woman. I said I would be delighted, and Madame Bernhardt invited us for tea. She was at the Great Northern Hotel in Chicago, where she occupied the whole top floor. (That was the only hotel in Chicago that would take her with all her animals, and she refused to be parted from them.) There she was with her dogs, baby leopard, cat and many birds. We arrived a little earlier than we were expected. Madame Bernhardt was not in, but as we rang the bell we heard the dogs bark and a great commotion inside. The door was opened and we were ushered into a large sitting room, in one corner of which was a table covered with more food than I had ever seen at any one time before, and I thought we were asked to a great party, but found out later that we were the only guests.

While we were waiting for Madame, my attention was drawn to a fluttering sound at one of the windows. It was so strong and forceful I thought it must be a window shade flapping in the wind, but in a partially covered parrot's cage there were three of the most distressed looking chickens I ever saw—about the size of good broilers. They had no feathers to speak of, but on the wing of one of them were a few bright red feathers; and I think somewhere on the second one there may have been a few feathers of blue. The other chicken had perfectly natural white feathers. As no one in the room spoke English except Madame Picard, I exclaimed, "For mercy's sake, ask the history of those chickens!" This was her reply: they were given to Madame on the Fourth of July as tiny baby chicks, and had been dyed—red, white and blue. She had been very much touched by the gift, and decided to keep them. So, ever since, the barnyard chicks had been traveling in the company of the dogs, cats, cubs and birds! Her maid said that Madame was very sentimental and could not possibly dispose of such a gift.

About this time Madame herself came in; it was like an entrance on a stage. All the animals showed their joy and the parrot said "Hello." I guess he said "hello." Whatever he said was in French, but it was a greeting. After she had patted the dogs and said a word to every one, we sat down for a little chat. She understood my English as well as I did her French; but dear Madame Picard was an able interpreter, and told me that Madame Bernhardt was genuinely interested in my music. She was delightfully encouraging, and told Madame Picard to say that if I ever came to Paris she would see that I met the right people to be of service to me.

Three years later she came to Chicago again. At this time there was some trouble with the theatrical syndicate, and Madame Bernhardt could not rent a theater, so a great tent was erected on the lake front and there she gave her plays. This time she was living in her private car, and again I went down to the railroad siding and sent in my card. It seemed rather strange

117

to go to call on her when I could not speak her language, but she had been so encouraging to me at the first meeting that I dared to try to see her again. I was able to make her understand that I was now getting on better, and was publishing my own songs. Through an interpreter she told me humorously of her difficulties with the organization that controlled the theaters, and she hoped the next time we met it would be in a theater. She went to the steps of the car with me and said good-by. Alas! Poor, divine Sarah! I have thought many times of how her appearance that day was anything but what a hero worshiper would imagine. Her whole costume, hair and face, were in disarray.

But the next time I saw her, a few years later on the stage of the Auditorium Theater, Madame's health was failing fast and she had to be considered and saved in every possible way. A great dressing room had been improvised for her on the stage of the theater. It was winter and they had made the room entirely of furs —walls, ceilings and floor, covered with beautiful furs. In the center of this room was a great divan of furs, and on this was Madame, resting.

She was dressed in a beautiful gown, the one she wore as La Tosca, and she was the most magnificent and striking figure I have ever seen. My mind went back to the steps of the private car on the lake front that cold afternoon, and I saw again the disheveled hair and ugly dress, and it was very hard for me to believe this beautiful figure was the same person. But in her eyes, her hands, and golden voice, and in her soul was that greatness which never changed nor died. No matter where she was nor what she wore, she was marvelous to behold. Her audience were the only people, I suppose, that she cared to dress up for—they furnished the only occasion that called for it. This time, in that furry, barbaric dressing room we did not talk. She took my hand; I stooped and kissed her. I never saw this incomparable artist of the indomitable heart again.

It was an American actress, though, who gave me the greatest encouragement, and one of my greatest opportunities—Margaret Anglin. I was introduced to her by Mr. and Mrs. Chauncey Olcott. Mr. Olcott had sung my songs, and he and his wife had always been my good friends.

The Roads of Melody

After our introduction, Miss Anglin invited me to come to her hotel for tea the next day. I no sooner entered her room than she said: "Now Mrs. Bond, what can I do to help you? I know all about your struggles, and that you have been pretty courageous, and I want to do something." "The only thing I want you to do is to like my music," I said. She pointed to the piano and said, "Well, play some little songs for me, will you?"

When I had finished she said, "All you need is to be heard."

"Oh, how I want my music to be known," I told her. "I seem to be able to arouse more enthusiasm from my songs by giving a program myself than by having other singers sing them."

"Of course," she answered. "You know more about your songs than any one else. Now, I have a little theater in New York called the Bijou, and I want to give you that theater for some recitals. I can promote three recitals for you. Will you come?" Would I!

In New York Miss Anglin had prevailed on three charities to participate, they to receive a

ELBERT HUBBARD

To Dear Carrie Jacobs Bond
with the affection & the
adoration of
Margaret Anglin.

MARGARET ANGLIN

percentage of the receipts; and though she was playing a strenuous rôle every night in the "Great Divide" with Henry Miller, she decorated the stage with her own hands each afternoon.

I think the help Miss Anglin gave me was greater than that given me by any other one person, and her friendship has ever since acted as an inspiration to me; but to this day she never wants me to speak about those wonderful afternoons in New York. Wonderful to me! Not only did these concerts net me several hundred dollars, but I gained a great deal of worth-while publicity. For the first time I did not have to look out for this side of the work myself. Miss Anglin sent her personal publicity man to me and had me meet the critics and all the reporters who wrote about happenings in musical affairs.

Those were great days for me. I was beginning now to be able to meet people who were of the greatest importance to my life, and it seemed to me that for a few years, I never walked; I ran! I was delivering songs and seeing music publishers and writing. It was now that I began writing the sketches of my "Old Man" series, which I had to write in order to make a varied program, feeling that my songs alone for a whole evening were a little monotonous. These little stories would never have seen the light of day had it not been for another remarkable woman friend, a famous writer of poems and stories, Mrs. Agnes Green Foster of Chicago. It was she who typed every poem for me, and who persuaded me to have them printed and made into a little book which I dedicated to her with great love. It was only a small edition—I think perhaps two hundred volumes—but it was her great encouragement and love that made these verses possible.

This Old Man about whom I wrote was a creature purely of imagination. I really knew no old-fashioned folks like my Old Man, but I often wished I had known them. I knew that such lived somewhere in the world. So in my dream I found a dear Old Man who had inherited one hundred acres of virgin forest. There he lived with his sweet, old wife; happy, just by themselves. He felled trees and made his own log house and she wove all the mats and curtains. They made their little garden together, and they had every need fulfilled. But they were poor, just rich in land—and in love. One day a group of real estate promoters came to buy fifty acres of this forest, saying they were going to put an interurban railway through from a great city thirty miles away and joining a little town that my Old Man knew and loved. He said it was impossible for him to part with any of his land, but was finally persuaded that it was the proper thing to do and was asked what price he fixed for his property. He could not tell; he had never bought anything and had never sold anything, and would leave it entirely to them. He felt perfectly sure they would be absolutely honest with him.

Now, it is a pretty bad person who takes advantage of you when you absolutely trust him, and these men felt that; so when they handed him a check, it was for full value—and a little more. He looked at it a moment, and said, "I cannot accept it." "Why? Is it not enough?" he was asked. "I did not know there was so much money in the world!" he replied. "But you see, Mary and I always divide things even, so you will have to make it out in two checks." That was how my Old Man became wealthy. At last it was possible for him to take the journey around the world that he had always longed to take, and that was how he came to write the verses that were promoted by my friend Mrs. Foster. My Old Man had always been a poet at heart, and he wrote these little rimes to read to Mary.

He took the journey around the world—Mary refusing to go because she wanted to stay at home so he would have something to come back to. His words of greeting on his return were, "I've got home." He came into his house on the day of his return as though he had never been away, and he took Mary by the hand. They went out to the little garden and through the wicker gate and so on to the woodpile, and sat down on the sawbuck where they had sat together so many times to talk things over. As they sat there in the twilight they thought they heard the strains of "Home, Sweet Home," and the Old Man told Mary his little verse:

> *Been a-travelin' 'most a year,*
> *Been a powerful ways from here,*
> *Seen some sights I won't forget,*
> *Heard some sounds I'm hearing yet,*
> *But now I'm home.*

Sunny Slopes

Been to cities strange and new,
Some I liked, but just a few;
Still there's none of 'em can be
What this old farm is to me,
    'Cause it's my home.

There's my axe beside the tree—
Seems to sort o' beckon me;
Wonder if I've clean forgot
How to sliver off a knot—
    Since I left home?

How I'm lovin' every sound!
Acorns droppin' on the ground
Sounds like music to my ear,
Kind o' singing joy and cheer
    'Cause I've got home.

Is there anything so good
As bein' home—an' understood?
Folks don't criticize your ways
Where they've known you all your days—
    Right in your home.

Well, I'm thanking God for this—
I've been liked (enough to miss)
In the place I love the best,
An' I've just come back to rest,
    An' stay at home.

CHAPTER IV

NEW FRIENDS AND FACES

AGAIN it was kind friends who arranged a concert for me at the White House. I received the invitation from President and Mrs. Roosevelt; they were entertaining Joel Chandler Harris, better known as Uncle Remus. He was a very shy and modest man, and no one but the family was invited to the dinner for that reason. I arrived a little later and was ushered into the red room. There I sat in my lace dress which had been just a little changed since I had worn it in London. This time I think I had added a new blue velvet sash and a scarf of blue chiffon. I sat there in an agony of nervousness. Finally, I looked about the room at the pictures and behind me saw a portrait of Abraham Lincoln. That picture gave me courage. I thought, "You were plain and angular too, but nobody seemed to mind." With those thoughts my anxiety was entirely conquered, so that by the time the President and Mrs. Roosevelt came in I felt quite comfortable. Mrs. Roosevelt said, "I am sorry Mr. Harris is not going to join us. He said he would like to listen from the next room."

We went into the blue room and I sat at the piano, sang and played my children's songs, and again I was singing the "Captain of the Broom Stick Cavalry," when across the polished floor I saw dear Mr. Harris. As he came to the piano he said, "I came in because that is the kind of music I can understand." He sat down close to the piano. Among other songs I sang that night was one that had these words in it: "It ain't so much the doing, as the way the thing is did." As I sang these words, President Roosevelt came over to the piano, put his hand on mine, stopped the song and said, "Mrs. Bond, you will never say any truer words than those." As I said good-by to them that night Mrs. Roosevelt explained to me that the President had been terribly hurt that day by the act of a friend, that it was not the thing that was done that had hurt him, but it was the way. That great man said he had enjoyed the evening. In a few days I received

an autographed picture of President Roosevelt—
one of my priceless possessions.

My next experience at the White House was
during the presidency of Mr. Harding. For
years "A Perfect Day" had been the favorite song
of the President and Mrs. Harding. Mr. Joe
Chapple, an intimate friend of theirs, told me of
this, and said he thought it would be nice if I
wrote a letter to the Hardings thanking them for
their interest—which I did. This was before the
President was in the White House. I received a
very gracious letter from President Harding,
written in his own hand, and by the same mail
came autographed pictures of the President and
Mrs. Harding.

From this time on, I was sent many, many
clippings (although I have never subscribed to
a clipping agency), about different occasions
where the song was sung or used at the White
House. The Marine Band always played it as
a closing number. A year or so after Mr.
Harding went to the White House, I was in
Washington on my way to Europe. It was the
year before the President's death. I sent a message asking if I might see the President. Months

before I had a very happy hour with Mrs. Harding, but the President was not in at the time. Shortly after my message was received an invitation was sent from them inviting me to bring my friends, Governor and Mrs. Yates, whom I was then visiting, and come to the concert at the White House that evening, after the dinner which they were giving for the Supreme Court judges.

As we entered, the Marine Band was playing "A Perfect Day," which was the last number on their program.

When Mrs. Harding came into the room she was evidently looking for me, and before she received her other guests, she made us more than happy and comfortable by introducing us to Judge Taft and his wife, with whom we spent the first few moments before the concert that was to be given in the blue room. I went into the music room just after the President and Mrs. Harding and sat directly back of them. We were handed programs for this beautiful concert, and the last number to be sung was "A Perfect Day." It was not done in my honor, because they did not know I was to be in Washington when the programs were printed. Just before the last group was sung, Mrs. Harding said, "Mrs. Bond, would you mind singing something for us?" The request was unexpected and I would have much preferred not to, but I did not see how I could refuse. After the program was over, I went to the piano and sang a group of songs. I have never ceased to be glad that I did, because it was my last meeting with President and Mrs. Harding.

On their way home from Alaska, when they arrived in San Francisco, Mr. Joe Chapple met them and was with them when the President died. He came down to Los Angeles bearing a message for Mr. Frank Miller and for me. The message was to tell Mr. Miller that the President had expected to go to Riverside to spend an hour with him, and that Mrs. Harding was to have spent an hour with me in my Hollywood home. My song, "A Perfect Day," was sung by Mrs. Harding's request, at her funeral.

In the beginning I never had any real belief in my own verses. I wrote them simply because I did not know any other way to secure lyrics, having no money to buy them; but a friend happened to send me a newspaper with the words of the poem "Just a Wearyin' for You." There was no author's name and I had no idea of copyrights or the right to use things which were already printed, and supposed in my ignorance that poems without any name, especially if they appeared in a newspaper, could be used by any one. It was not so very long afterward that I learned better, but the music for "Just a Wearyin'" had been printed and published when I discovered that the poem was written by Frank L. Stanton, and that it had appeared in a book published by D. Appleton and Company, of New York. I was very much excited and wondered who in the world could advise me what to do. I thought of John McCutcheon, whose sister Jessie and I were very dear friends, as I felt sure he would know the publishers. To him I went and told him my story. He said, "I think the best thing for you to do is to go to New York and see Mr. Appleton. I know him personally and will give you a letter, and I am very sure when he hears your story he will believe you. You are not going to have any difficulty."

But I had been told about law suits; of the awful things that happen to people who plagiarize other people's ideas, and by this time it looked to me as though I were a criminal. You know it doesn't make any difference how ignorant you are; if there is proof that you did it, that is about all that is necessary; and I *had* published somebody's poem without giving him credit, or even asking permission.

I remember it took pretty nearly all the money I had to pay the expenses to New York. I sat up all night in the chair car and carried my luncheon. Fortunately, I met Mr. Appleton immediately; I told him the story and asked him if there were any possible way in which I could settle the matter. He assured me that my crime was forgivable, that they owned the little poem—they had bought all rights—and that I was perfectly welcome to it! You can imagine the comfort that gave me.

But before I knew of this, I had committed the same sort of crime with a verse called "Poor Little Lamb," which I found in the same way, without any author. Shortly after this experience with Mr. Appleton, and before I had a chance to find out where the author, Paul Lawrence Dunbar, lived, I received a letter from him saying he would like to see me; and I made an appointment. At that meeting he said, "Mrs. Bond, you are using one of my verses without my permission." I must say here that he had the most wonderful speaking voice I have ever heard. I told him then of my ignorance and of my other difficulties. We talked of our troubles, told each other some sad experiences, and when he left I decided that Paul Lawrence Dunbar's life was the saddest of any I had ever known. I can hear his voice yet as he said: "I really think I shall be glad when it is all over." He was silent for a long while and then he asked: "Would you mind playing me that song you wrote for my verses?"—which I did. Then he said: "I am going to let you have it under one condition, and that is that you will write the music for a cycle I have just completed." A few days later he brought to me two poems called "Love and Sorrow" and "The Las' Long Res'."

I have often wondered if my friendship for Paul Lawrence Dunbar created a serious situation, which almost brought a libel suit against a a religious paper. I was visiting in the home of Mrs. Charles Modini Wood of Los Angeles when her little girl Mona came home from school in great excitement. When she was calm enough to tell us what it was all about, this is what she said: The teacher had given them "Poor Little Lamb" to sing, giving them both the names of the poet and the composer, and saying to the children that it is a most extraordinary thing that both the poet and composer are Negroes. Little Mona said right out in school, "She's my Auntie Bond and she is not black. She is visiting in my mother's house to-day." The Los Angeles school-teacher, however, was not so easily dissuaded by this correction from her pupil and went on to tell her children to be as nice as they could to Negroes because often they were really brilliant. This story grew and grew and was part of a tremendous quantity of dramatic fiction when "The End of a Perfect Day" was published. In a small religious journal there appeared an editorial comment:

It is not generally known that the composer of "The End of a Perfect Day" is a colored woman. She is Mrs. Carrie Jacobs-Bond and is her own publisher. The *American Musician* says Mrs. Bond has received more from this composition than she can spend extravagantly the balance of her life.

We considered suing. The paper had only about eleven or twelve thousand subscribers— almost exclusively ministers—but it was the sort of paper people take on faith. No one expects the religious press to take such flyers into the realm of sensation. Editors everywhere had reprinted this story. We pursued the matter and secured some seventy-five or eighty retractions, and then let the matter drop.

One day I went down to Orchestra Hall to meet Mr. Wessels, then the manager of the Chicago Symphony Orchestra. After we had had a little talk about my music he said, "David Bispham is going to give a concert next week; I will be glad to introduce you. Bring down some of your songs, meet him, and see if you can get his interest in them." This invitation I was very glad to accept. I heard a fine concert and then Mr. Wessels introduced me to Mr. Bispham. I had my little package of songs with me. By this time I had published about fifty. I brought to him the book *Seven Songs* and the book called

Eleven Songs. (Here I might remark that I have written twelve books of songs.)

Mr. Bispham accepted the songs and said, "I will be glad to look them over; you will hear from me later. It may not be at once, but I promise you I will look them over carefully."

A year went by and again I was in London. While there I picked up a paper one morning and saw Mr. David Bispham's name. I secured his address and telephone number and called him up. He seemed cordial and glad to hear from me, and asked if I cared to come over that afternoon. He said he would be very glad to talk over the songs, and that I might listen to a rehearsal; also that he was singing some new songs by an English composer and thought it would be interesting to me to be there. After hearing Mr. Bispham sing these songs of his friend, I was asked if I would sing a group of my songs for them. By this time I had become accustomed to doing my songs for great musicians and was less frightened than formerly. When I left Mr. Bispham he said, "I shall be in America before long and will certainly sing one of your

MUSIC HALL

SUNDAY AFTERNOON, APRIL 2, 1905, at 3:30.

SONG RECITAL BY

MR. DAVID BISPHAM

AT THE PIANO,

Mrs. CARRIE JACOBS-BOND and Mr. HAROLD O. SMITH.

Direction F. WIGHT NEUMANN.

PROGRAM.

1. a. Ruddier Than The Cherry .... *Handel*
   b. Who's Sylvia? .... *Schubert*
   c. Creation's Hymn .... *Beethoven*

2. Nothing But a Wild Rose. From Three Songs
   Still Unimpressed
   The Las' Long Res' .... From Seven Songs
   Good Night
   In a Foreign Land.   MRS. CARRIE
   Just by Laughing. .... From Ten Songs...   JACOBS-BOND
   The Gate of Tears
   May I Print a Kiss"

3. a. The Two Grenadiers .... *Schumann*
   b. The Monk .... *Meyerbeer*

4. a. Where Youths' Eternal
   b. Linger Not.
   c. A Study in Symbols.
   d. Until God's Day .... From Eleven and   MRS. CARRIE
   e. The Lily and The Rose   Twelve Songs...   JACOBS-BOND
   f. The Greatest Charm.
   g. The Dear Awfuelswahn.

5. a. The Pretty Creature
   b. Drink To Me Only With Thine Eyes } *Old English*
   c. Young Richard

STEINWAY PIANO USED.

MUSIC HALL
Sunday Afternoon, April 2, at 3.30

DAVID BISPHAM
assisted by
MRS. CARRIE JACOBS-BOND
Under the Direction of F. WIGHT NEUMANN

THE BISPHAM PROGRAM

THE END OF THE ROAD, MY HOLLYWOOD HOME

IN THE GARDEN AT THE END OF THE ROAD, HOLLYWOOD

songs." A few months after that I did have a
cable from him and such a cable:

Giving concert in Studebaker Hall, Chicago.
I shall be very happy to sing fifteen of your songs,
and I wish you would accompany me.

I went straight down to Mr. Bispham's Chicago manager and told him what a great thing
had happened. I thought he would share my
enthusiasm, but he didn't. He said: "Mrs. Bond,
I am very sorry, but I think there must be some
mistake. I do not think Mr. Bispham could
possibly do that. In the first place, I think it
would be suicide for him to attempt such a thing
as to sing fifteen of your songs. It would not be
a success. I don't want to discourage you, but
I wouldn't count on it too much. You should
know that singers change their minds, and say
things sometimes to be agreeable."

But I never doubt people until I have to, and
I did not doubt Mr. Bispham's word for a moment. I believed he would do as he said, though
I questioned my ability to accompany him. Anyway, the manager assured me, there would be no
one there, and it would be an entire failure; he

was sorry. I never did believe that "sorry."

Although I had just one hundred dollars in the bank, with which I expected to buy my dress for this affair, as soon as the tickets were on sale for the concert I bought one hundred dollars' worth. I felt most uncomfortable when I thought of trying to sell these tickets to my friends, but I could not afford to give them all away. I think I sold about fifty. The next question was, What was I going to do for a dress? Among my acquaintances was a lady who used to live in Janesville, Miss Morissey, but who had been in Chicago for several years, and who was very well known as a wonderful dressmaker. I told her the story of the hundred dollars, and asked her if she would trust me for a dress. She did, and made for me one of the most beautiful dresses I ever owned. I shall never forget it. That was years ago when they put twenty-five yards of material into a dress; and it was all tucked and fluted and ruffled, combined with lace, and was quite magnificent. Up to this time, I had always made my own hats, but I felt now that I should go to a milliner for this one. This I did, taking some pieces of the dress to her, together with two lovely ostrich feathers, which looked very well.

The concert was to be on Sunday; late Saturday night I got my hat. I do not suppose I am any more vain than most women, but something told me early on Sunday morning to try on the dress and hat and see what I was going to look like in the afternoon. The dress was very becoming, but oh, that hat! I never could wear it! What in the world was I going to do? When I was in England the last time, in a very rash moment of extravagance, I had bought some lovely pink velvet roses which I had never worn. It was about ten o'clock in the morning when I began that hat of my own fabrication, and all that I had to work with were some pieces of lace and silk like those of the dress, and the wreath of pink velvet roses—no frame, no wire. But it did not take me long to take the wire out of the milliner's hat, and with some buckram and pasteboard, I made a frame that looked like me; at least, I felt that it did. I covered it with the material and put the wreath of roses on it. And it matched! No one but the cousin who was with me on that grand and glorious day ever knew

139

about that hat. Maybe the dress was so beautiful that no one noticed the rest of the costume.

Now when the time came for me to go to the piano, I felt that my trembling fingers would never find the keys. Out of the fifteen songs Mr. Bispham was to sing there was not one to be used in the original key, and I had to transpose them all. Between the anxiety of playing in a key I was not familiar with, and accompanying a great singer for the first time in my life, and being on the stage again, I wondered how it would be possible to go on. But the fifteen little songs were sung and I played them somehow. The hall was packed; people were standing and many were turned away. I was not so excited, however, but that I thought, "I wish I had never spent that hundred dollars; the tickets would have been sold anyway."

After the last song there was such applause as I had never heard. I did not raise my eyes, however; I did not dream that any of it was for me. I do not think I ever thought what it was all about; I was merely glad that I had played those fifteen songs without a mistake. But finally, after about five minutes of applause, Mr.

Bispham touched me on the shoulder and said, "Aren't you going to stand up pretty soon, Mrs. Bond? You know this is for you too." My heart seemed to burst with gratitude, not only to Mr. Bispham, but to that whole audience—all these people who were so kind and sympathetic. Chicago friends! For a good number of them were my friends, who had come for that very reason.

Mr. Bispham and I left the stage together, and he said, "You will have to go back and speak." Oh, I could not! "Then sing; sing 'The Captain of the Broom Stick Cavalry.'" I went to the piano but have always felt that no one heard my voice. I was so frightened and overcome with emotion, that I think I must have whispered that song.

When, at the end of that memorable concert, the manager who had been so pessimistic about the whole affair came to me back of the stage and took my hand and excitedly exclaimed, "Mrs. Bond, you are made!" my kind friend, Mr. Bispham said, "Yes, but not by this afternoon!"

David Bispham never failed to be a loyal friend. He sang "The End of a Perfect Day" the first time it was ever sung by any one but me, and I always went to him with all my new things and he would encourage me. He was always interested in everything I wrote and made but one little criticism that I recall. He said he thought there should be a little more interlude between the two verses of "A Perfect Day"—something I improvised in his presence then and there, and he approved of it.

Of course, David Bispham was just such a friend to hundreds of others. He always had time to do kind things and to help struggling people, and he did it in such a way that one felt he was glad to do it, and I think he was. When he died, the world lost a great musician, and I lost a noble friend.

CHAPTER V

JOURNEY'S END

UST before Mr. Walter Gale came into the business I asked my son to give up his engineering and come with me. It did not seem a very big business, to be sure, but I was making my expenses and about forty dollars a month, and I felt positive that the profits could be greater if there was some one with a business head to look after it. That, I felt sure, my son had, for he had taken care of himself entirely for three years and helped me besides.

With true unselfishness my son left the eighth grade before he was thirteen, refusing to go to school again and insisting upon going to work to help his mother—which he did. Shortly after this he was taken very ill and was in the County Hospital for almost three months. County hospitals are wonderful places, but it seemed quite terrible for me, although at one time I myself had been ill in the County Hospital for several weeks. But there I had to leave him, and from that time on, hospitals were to play quite a part in my life.

After his recovery my health broke and I spent many weeks of the coming years in hospitals. First, it was twelve weeks in the Chicago Hospital; a few years after that, eight weeks in St. Luke's, to say nothing of the weeks I spent in Christine Forsythe's Sanitarium. But during those years I came in close contact with many physicians and surgeons who showed me the greatest courtesy, as the widow of a physician. All this must have been in return for the many kind deeds of my husband. I am glad that I believe absolutely in the law of compensation, and that sometime, somewhere, there is always a reward for every kind deed. Maybe those who do the kindness do not personally receive it back again, but I believe it is passed on to some one they love, which perhaps makes the reward even greater.

To go back to my son—when he left the eighth grade he immediately took up night school work and decided that he wanted to be a civil engineer. All this time he was at work and giving me every dollar. When it was no longer convenient for him to attend night school he started a course in engineering with a correspondence school, and in a few years he was a graduate engineer, passing with honors.

I was singing in Burlington, Iowa, when I met Mrs. Perkins, whose husband was the President of the Burlington Railroad. She had taken quite an interest in my career and invited me to spend an afternoon with her. I found she was very much interested in my welfare. She had been told that my boy was ill and wanted to know if there was not something she could do for him. You see, fate had always turned around to help me, just as in this case. At that time I did not know that her husband was the President of the Burlington road, but I said, "The doctor told me that my son must go immediately into the country from this hospital. He is quite well now but he must be out of doors for at least three months. I had been thinking that such an opportunity would come along, for he is a civil engineer and that would keep him out of doors." "Why, of course," she said, "I can make it possible. If he were here he could start to-morrow with a company from the Burlington office. My husband, who is the President of the Burlington Railroad, is constantly putting out young engineers, and they begin at forty dollars a month. We will telegraph for your boy." We sent for him and for the next three years he was away from home most of the time.

But to go back to Fred and me as partners in the Bond Shop. Ledgers, journals, rulers and erasers, files and all the other office paraphernalia which he had noticed in the railroad offices were now purchased; and my son began a very watchful, careful study of how to make the Bond Shop produce money. Very soon we outgrew the dining room in the little apartment at 5455 Drexel Avenue. We had a good-sized sign painted reading THE BOND SHOP. After having it made we found we would not be allowed to put it outside on the apartment building, so, although no one could see it, we hung up the sign in the dining room and made ourselves think we had a little business office. The business grew until we were clearing about one hundred and fifty dollars a month. Now we really did need more room and we gave over the entire apartment of five rooms

THE BOND SHOP IN THE DINING ROOM, 1914

SHIPPING ROOM OF THE BOND SHOP, COLONNADE BUILDING, CHICAGO

Our One-Room Mansion

to the Bond Shop. Soon, that was not nearly large enough, so we moved to seven rooms in the same building. My son seemed to be the mascot we had been looking for; of course, it really was that he had a fine business ability. I had created the demand and was constantly creating it afresh, but now things were being managed as it had been absolutely impossible for me to manage them, and everything looked brighter.

At this time Mr. Walter Gale came into the business, as I have already mentioned, and he decided that we should have a storeroom. Accordingly, we rented a back room of a pharmacy on North Michigan Boulevard, and here, at last, we were able to put out the Bond Shop sign where it would show. Business, indeed, was picking up and now we had to have a delivery wagon. It is amusing to recall, but at the time it was with the greatest pride I saw my son tie bundles of sheet music on the back of a motorcycle, perhaps five hundred or a thousand copies, and start off down town to deliver these wares to the different music stores. Pretty soon we had to buy a motor cycle with a side car; and where it had been perhaps one thousand copies a little while ago, it was now five thousand. We then decided to move down town, so we went to housekeeping in the seven rooms and hired a room in the Chicago Musical College Building, with our name not only on the front door but on the elevator directory in the hall. I believe this was in 1908. From then on, things began to go more smoothly.

After a year we moved to the Fine Arts Building, where, though we had just one room, it was a fine one. It was here that "A Perfect Day" was first published. Partitions made three rooms —bookkeeping department, shipping department as well as general office, and Fred had a little mahogany roll-top desk inside a railing in one corner of the room, which became a private office. We were now employing several people.

At this juncture my son was taken ill again, I think this time from overwork and worry, and was compelled to take a rest. He went to the country for two weeks, and during that period I decided for the first time to make a move of my own accord. While he was away, I rented a space of five thousand feet in the Old Colonnade Building, and had everything in pretty good order when my son returned. I have never seen him so surprised over anything. I think he was a little anxious about it, for this was incurring a great deal of extra expense; but something told me— I guess it was my good fairy—that we were going to need all this room. And so events proved.

Later, we moved to the corner section of the Colonnade Building where we occupied eight thousand feet of space. That one song should necessitate moving to larger quarters may seem strange to the reader, but the reader probably does not know the amount of stock it is necessary to keep on hand when one has at last found one-self possessor of a popular song. It was not just the song alone; there were some sixty different ar-rangements of "The End of a Perfect Day," among them, the ukulele, banjo, guitar, mandolin, accordion, pipe organ; for male and female voices, mixed voices, quartettes, trios; concert pianists, military bands, concert bands, piano and guitar, piano and cornet, piano and viola, piano and flute, piano and violin, piano and cello, solo cello, and many others. We had these filed in a way that took up a great deal of room, but they were so filed that a stranger coming into the Bond Shop could have found within five minutes any piece of music, or the arrangement of it, he wished. The Bond Shop used to be pointed out in the trade as a model music shop.

I always was, and shall always be, proud of this accomplishment. My son did so much, and he started without having been trained in the music business. The little shop that was started in the corner of a room grew to the point where we were employing seventeen people. Some of the things we did, even after we attained some little success, showed a general inaptitude for a business or a publishing life.

In the year 1909 there was enacted a law by Congress which made it obligatory for the various recording companies to pay royalties to the publishers on copyright music which they recorded. It was fixed that a royalty of not less than two cents must be paid upon every copy manufactured. There was an allowance for breakage, of course. I was approached by one of the companies to make a record of "The End of a Perfect Day." This same company had already made some records of some of my earlier songs, and I had liked their work, so I granted exclusive right to them to make "The End of a Perfect Day."

When another company asked for permission to record the song, and sent us a contract to sign, I returned it, telling them that I had given the exclusive right to their rival. So they went ahead and announced a rendition of my song. We were just ready to proceed against them legally, when we discovered that once permission had been given for the recording of a song, it was given automatically to any one else who might wish to record it. The publisher cannot distinguish between competing companies. Soon we corrected our mistake and signed the second contract. There were, I believe, nearly fifty recordings of one sort or another made of this one song, but I believe the first fine record of "A Perfect Day" was sung by Mr. Evan Williams. He made also the first record of "A Little Bit of Honey," which was the last record he made for the Victor Company.

The first time I played my song, "A Perfect Day," for my son, he was in Hollywood. He said very simply, but with a good deal of conviction, "Mother, you have written a success."

It may be of interest to my readers to know how I happened to come to California, and how I happened to write "A Perfect Day." For many, many weeks I had been very ill in the Chicago Hospital. It was just after Christmas and my physician and friend, Dr. Alexander Ferguson of Chicago, said, "Mrs. Bond, you must go away to a warmer climate; that is absolutely necessary. You will find some way, I am sure." He had done everything he could for me. I feel I owe my life to the genius of Dr. Ferguson.

But where to go? And how to leave the business? In the midst of this questioning a friend came in to see me and I told her what the doctor had said.

"Is that not strange?" she said. "I have been visiting friends who are very much interested in your work. In fact, I have an engagement for you to open their music house on their estate in the spring." She mentioned the name of Mr. W. H. Minor, owner of that magnificent model farm——Heart's Delight Farm in Chazy, New York. Of course, that was a journey and a change, although it could not be made until spring. "But while we were speaking of you," my friend went on, "Mr. Minor wondered if you would like to take a trip to California. He said there were some fine opportunities there for people like you to earn their transportation and have a few days there with all expenses paid. The Santa Fe Railroad is opening reading rooms and gymnasiums for its employees, and it is offering this as an inducement for artists who would like to make a journey like that, by giving them the trip in return for recitals."

How wonderful it seemed, and through Mr. Minor I was immediately put in touch with Mr. Busser of the Santa Fe Railroad. I was told that the company would be very happy to arrange a tour for me.

I think I gave eight recitals on the trip. At that time the Santa Fe did not have the beautiful reading rooms and little theaters it now has for its employees. Sometimes I gave a recital in a church, but all the railroad people and any one else who cared to come were welcome. It was all free. I remember being obliged after every one of these recitals to send for a doctor to be straightened out for the next lap of the journey. When I arrived in California and sent for Dr. Duffield, an old-time friend, he said he wondered how I had lived to complete the journey.

More good luck was waiting for me. In those first few days in California I met Madame Genevra Johnstone Bishop, a famous Chicago singer, and sister of my devoted friends, Mr. and Mrs. Homer Johnstone. She was singing at the Hollywood Hotel, arranging recitals for Sunday evening concerts, and the first Sunday I was in California she invited me to come to the hotel and asked if I would mind singing some of my songs on her program, which I did. This was the beginning of a very sincere friendship with Mrs. Anderson—she who made the Hollywood Hotel famous, and inspired so many to build their homes in Hollywood, then a little village.

I remember this old Hollywood and love the memory. It was a beautiful place, at the foot of the mountains, looking across a wide valley of oil fields to its maternal city, beautiful Los Angeles. Not much of a city, though, twenty-five years ago! In Hollywood I recall just a few lovely homes, among them Paul DeLongpre's, the painter, who had a magnificent garden on Hollywood Boulevard, a corner of which is now worth several millions; the hotel on Highland Avenue and Hollywood Boulevard; across the way a bank

MISSION INN, RIVERSIDE, CALIFORNIA, WHERE "A PERFECT
DAY" WAS WRITTEN

NESTOREST, MY LITTLE COTTAGE IN GOD'S GARDEN,
GROSSMONT, CALIFORNIA

MY FAITHFUL FRIENDS, MICHAEL AND POOCH

and a drug store. It was a village of horse cars and dirt roads. There was one crossroad, Vermont Avenue, which was the short cut from Los Angeles to Hollywood. It was not so very short, as it was rough and bumpy; but it was always beautiful because of its lovely trees.

In those days no one dreamed what Hollywood was going to grow into. We all thought it would be a beautiful home place; of course, it was that already; but I have lived to see Los Angeles pass its million mark and Hollywood become a city of more than one hundred and seventy-five thousand people, and however much maligned, one of the most beautiful and interesting cities in the world, a place I am proud to call my home.

The only wish I have is that people who have believed the things they have heard about it could live in it for a few years. Almost every city of any importance has things happen in it for which the citizens grieve, but every city does not have the publicity which our Hollywood has. I am told that it is a matter of good business—this publicity—but I am sorry it is.

From this first evening at the Hollywood Hotel

came a future. That evening it was arranged that I should come every winter and live at the Hollywood Hotel, arrange the concerts for Sunday evening and sing once a month myself, for which I was to receive my room and board. The Santa Fe Railroad Company said I might sing my way to California indefinitely, and I did that for about six years. It was a delightful experience in every way. I found to my great surprise that by singing at the Hollywood Hotel I was giving greater publicity to my music than I could ever have done in any other way, and very much more easily. Every winter I planned to come to Mrs. Anderson for two months. This was not only a good business deal, but was probably the salvation of my health.

The story of the writing of "The End of a Perfect Day" has been told many, many times, and in many, many ways, but the truth is a very simple story. The inspiration came to me as I was viewing a wonderful sunset from the top of Mt. Rubidoux in Riverside, California, this glorious place that has been made famous by the Easter morning sunrise services, inaugurated by Frank Miller, Master of the Mission Inn. I had been motoring through Southern California with some nature-loving friends; we had been seeing many beautiful sights, but the glory of this sunset from the mountain was the most beautiful thing I had ever seen.

I hurried back to the Mission Inn to get ready for dinner, and while dressing I thought how I wished I could express my thanks to those friends in some little way, just out of the ordinary; and almost at once came the words for "A Perfect Day." I wrote them very hurriedly; I did not have time to change a word or a sentence. I took them down and read them at the dinner that evening, then put them in my purse and thereupon forgot them.

About three months later I was crossing the Mohave Desert, in the moonlight, with some more nature-loving friends; and without realizing that I had memorized those words, I began singing them to the original tune. My friend, Mrs. Hawks, who sat next to me, and in whose home I had spent many happy days, whose loving interest had encouraged me to write so many songs, said, "Carrie, you have another song, haven't you?" "Well," I replied, "maybe I have." I stayed in her home that night, but did not go to sleep. I finished the song entirely before morning.

And that is the true story of "A Perfect Day."

The story that has become so widely known, and which I think is very interesting but entirely untrue, is that I was with my husband on my honeymoon; that we were in Switzerland and had climbed to one of the highest peaks in the Alps at sunset; and that, in my wild enthusiasm, being a most erratic musician, I impulsively threw my arms around my husband and pushed him over the cliff; that he was killed instantly; and that I rushed back to the hotel and immediately wrote "This Is the End of a Perfect Day."

I have heard a great many other stories, enough of them to fill a big book; but this, I think, is the funniest one.

To go back to beautiful Mt. Rubidoux. Later I wrote an anthem to be sung at the Easter morning service. Six hundred people had been brought from Los Angeles by Mr. Carl Bronson, who was to direct their singing of the anthem. A full band from Riverside was to accompany them and

Madame Marcella Craft was the soloist. The orchestra and the choir arrived at the top of the mountain in plenty of time, but the crowd was so dense that Mr. Bronson, the director, was not able to get through, and as the sun does not wait for any one, it commenced to rise and the anthem had to be sung as the sun was rising. Evidently, those people thought they could sing without a director. The band began and so did the singers, but not within two bars were they together. The band was playing as well as it could, and as loudly, and the singers were doing their best. I was just far enough away to be able to hear the most awful discords I had ever heard in my life. I walked straight up that perpendicular hill, cried to those singers, "Stop! Stop!" Of course they could not hear me, but they saw me waving my hands wildly and stop they did. The band saved the day and Marcella Craft sang the solo beautifully; but I think it was one of my most embarrassing moments.

I have heard also that there was a most wonderfully romantic experience connected with my writing of "A Perfect Day" which had nothing to do with my husband. I have had strangers

look me right in the eye and say: "Mrs. Bond,
won't you tell us what made you write 'The End
of a Perfect Day?' Was it really a love affair?"
I have often thought how terrible it would be if
something like that really had inspired the song.
I should have had to look some one straight in
the eye and say, "Oh, don't ask me."

Of course, because you write songs that are
tender and sometimes songs of love, it does not
follow, as so many people think it does, that every
one of these songs is the result of a personal
experience. People with imagination can have a
lot of fun just thinking about things.

But, of course, I have written some songs that
meant the whole world to me—like "The Hand
of You"—when I was homesick for my boy:

Sometimes when shadows cross my path
As shadows sometimes do,
I reach my hand across the mist,
And touch the hand of you.

I know the sun is in the sky,
I know true love is true;
But, oh, it comforts in the dark,
To touch the hand of you.

Journey's End

Through all the silence of the years,
Through friendships old and new
The dearest memory of my life,
I touched the hand of you.

So clouds and sorrows come along,
We all must have a few,
But through them all, please God, let me
Still touch the hand of you.

Or "Homeland," when I longed for my own
country:

The blue-bells and the butter-cups,
Are bloss'ming on the lea;
But poppy fields and lupin hills,
Are what I want to see.

The chestnut trees are white with bloom,
For miles along the way;
But 'cacia trees with tips of gold,
Are what I miss to-day.

A thrush is gaily singing,
In a lovely cypress tree;
But oh! I wish a mocking bird,
Would come and sing to me.

The Roads of Melody

I'm lonely and my heart is sad,
No longer would I roam;
I'm longing for my native land,
I'm homesick for my home.

I want to see the friends I love,
The folks who understand,
Be in a world a little new,
Near miles of untouch'd land.

Close to the desert of my soul,
Where strangeness never jars,
In blessed California,
'Neath the flag of stripes and stars.

When "A Perfect Day" was successfully launched, I began to receive a series of letters from a woman in Missouri, who threatened to take action against me. She contended that we were pirating her original verse of "A Perfect Day." She assured me through her attorney that she had written it. After about fifteen or twenty of these letters had come through her attorney, I finally decided to have the matter looked into. My son located the husband of the woman, who told him that practically every publisher in the country had been to see him, that his wife was mentally unbalanced and that she had claimed authorship of "The Rosary" and several other songs as well as my "End of a Perfect Day."

Again, one day at the Beverly Hills Hotel, I had been singing the song and a lady came up to me with a letter in her hand, saying, "I have just received this letter from the gentleman who wrote the words of 'A Perfect Day.'"

After "The End of a Perfect Day" was written, and affairs were becoming easier financially, I purchased my first automobile, a little electric machine, one of those lovely roomy ones with a great, big top that could be put up and down, and with electric lights on each side. They would look absurd to us now, those old chariots, but they were quite elegant at that time.

I bought this as a surprise for my son, who was coming to visit me in California, and I was practicing every day, because I intended to drive to the station to meet him. The first time I drove down town I was crossing one of the busiest streets in Los Angeles when the policeman held up his hand as the signal to stop. Not being quite comfortable in the crowd, I did not stop just where I should have, and my electric ran over the crossing about ten feet. The policeman rushed up to me in a very dramatic manner and said, "Back up!"

I looked back, and I knew it was going to be an impossible thing for me to back up with any certainty of being able to stop before I hit some one, so I said, "I can't." He said, "You will!"

We had quite a little conversation with just those few words. By this time a crowd began to collect. Finally the policeman said, "You will back up or I will take you to jail." By that time the jail looked like a haven to me, so I rejoined, "Get in the car and I will take you there."

I did, expecting, of course, to find a kind judge sitting on the bench waiting to hear my story, which I felt was a perfectly good one. I felt as if I had probably saved some one's life by not backing up. I never had been in jail before, however, and when I got there I found I was to stay there until two o'clock in the afternoon, as that was the time the judge came in.

"Well, what are you going to do with me now?" I asked. "You can pay your bail or stay here," the policeman said. My bail was five dollars and I did not have my purse. "Can't you let me leave the machine?" I asked. I did not remember that it took ten cents to get to Hollywood on the street car. He answered, "No!" I happened to have on a diamond ring. "Would you take this?" I asked. "No!" With that, a kind-hearted policeman from the back of the room stepped up. "Madam," he said, "I will lend you five dollars until this afternoon." Which he did. How often have I wished I had the name of that policeman! It seems they were all joking each other about this. The poor policeman who had brought me to jail probably never had the least idea of doing it, but he could not do anything else but get in the car, with the crowd laughing as they were.

One reads a good many stories about "my most embarrassing moment"; but I know this was one more for me.

Well, after the excitement, thanking the man for his five dollars, and bailing myself out, I thought I had better telephone for a lawyer. I knew only one in Los Angeles, but I called the office of Albert Stevens. I believe he thought I had been arrested for some terrible crime because he arrived at the jail breathless to see what he could do for me. He tried not to let me see his smile when I told him. "Now don't be excited," he calmed me; "just get in your electric, drive home and forget it."

Well, I drove to the home of a friend and told her of the disgraceful thing that had happened to me. I stayed with her until evening. I was living in the Hollywood Hotel at the time, and when I went to the desk for my key at seven o'clock, the clerk said, "Mrs. Bond, where have you been all day? And what in the world has happened? Reporters waited here for hours, but finally got tired and went away. What is it all about?" Only then I thought, "Oh, mercy's sake, the newspapers!" Sure enough; the next morning, in pretty good-sized letters in the *Times*—with the cartoon of a frightened lady in an electric, with the hand of the law as big as the car held up in front of her—there it was: CARRIE JACOBS-BOND ARRESTED. And then, in very small type, the reason was stated. I called my friend Mrs. Hawkes and said, "Will you go to Grossmont with me? I am leaving early in the morning." She asked me for how long and I told her I had no idea. "Well, she said, "I can go for a few days." I, myself, hid away for two weeks.

In the meantime, back in Chicago, my son as he was riding to his office, opened his *Chicago Tribune* and he too saw in good-sized letters the headline: CARRIE JACOBS-BOND ARRESTED IN LOS ANGELES. He was so excited he could not read, and he handed the paper to a man who sat next to him, asking, "Would you mind telling me what this is about? I don't feel well." The other read the story of the poor old mother in disgrace. How he laughed! He may have thought it funny, but it was many years before it looked so funny to me.

Reverend Robert J. Burdett wrote a little poem about me in which he said: "Composer fails to find melody in policeman's whistle." He told me how I had said that Chicago policemen were polite; that they always said "please"; and that if this policeman had spoken to me in a Chicago manner none of this trouble would have happened.

The Roads of Melody

Of course my son telegraphed me a sympathetic message, but he immediately appreciated the value of the publicity of all this to the Bond Shop. It was not until 1922, when he and I were the guests of honor of the Advertising Club of Los Angeles, that I learned that he had been responsible for all of the publicity I had received. He told the story of my arrest, how he had secured permission of the *Chicago Tribune* to reprint that story, and how he had had copies of it sent out everywhere. We received stories from England and quantities of mail from the United States; many letters from people asking for money—asking me to buy for them pianos, and other trifles. One English woman asked me to advance her ten thousand dollars to buy a rooming house which, she felt sure, could repay her debt in a short time. By the time this story had been published a few times the editors had made me one of America's richest women, and the consequence was that these letters I mentioned, with their impossible requests, became a flood. Finally I thought things had gone far enough and I telegraphed my son to have our lawyer take steps to ascertain who was sending out these stories, but of course my son never could learn the identity of the sender.

I am well acquainted now with the great need of publicity, but I do not like it any better than I did twenty-five years ago. Of course the publicity I had had was of a very innocent nature, and funny. Probably much funnier because I took it so seriously.

I should like to mention the very first great newspaper publicity I was ever given. It was through the kindness of the late General Otis that in 1908 an entire page was given to my little Bond Shop in the Los Angeles *Times,* which he owned.

During this time I had become very tired of "The End of a Perfect Day"—of too many cartoons and pictures that seemed to strike me as most unnecessary, such as "This Is the End of a Perfect Day," with a picture of a road and five or six people staggering along so intoxicated they could not see where they were going; or a crowd of drunkards falling out of a taxi, all singing "This Is the End of a Perfect Day."

It was the war that made this a serious song to me. It was meant to be a happy song, but it has been used in some of the saddest episodes of my life; and its other side has been plainly marked to me. It was sung at the funeral of my dear friend, Walter Gale. It had always been loved by him. It was sung by me all through the war, and I received hundreds of letters, sad letters, from "Over There." I should like to quote many of those letters, but I cannot. However, there was one which ran: "Yesterday was a wonderful and terrible day to me. I went over the top for the first time. We were all inspired to do it, and we never realized anything about what it would be to meet the Germans. We simply marched on. When I had gone over and come back, I remember running as fast as I could back to my bunk, and I heard a voice and that voice was singing 'This Is the End of a Perfect Day'—and it was my voice. I have just time to write this little note to you to tell you that that song must have encouraged me to live."

In another letter there was a clipping from Glasgow from a dear mother who said, "My son has made the great sacrifice—Jamie has gone— he was buried yesterday. The last time we saw our boy he was waving his cap to us and he was marching away never to come back; and as he was looking at me he was singing 'The End of a Perfect Day.' "

Then, there was a letter from Ireland—from little Jean Craig—who gave up her stenographic work to sing for the boys in the hospitals. We corresponded for a long time during the war, and though I never saw or heard her, I know she must have been a sweet, sweet singer.

This is one of the stories she wrote me: She had gone into the hospital where the boys had been taken who had been wounded on the battle-ships by bombs, and one boy whom she remembered had asked her to sing. She sang "This Is the End of a Perfect Day." The boy asked her if she knew any more songs by Mrs. Bond and she replied that she did not. "Well," he said, "I'm going to die and I want to give you something; this is the one little treasure I have." With that he took from under his pillow a little book of *Seven Songs*. He had carried it inside his jacket all during his service; he had been rescued from the water and the leaves of the book were water-soaked; but as he gave it to Miss Craig he said: "I have taken the best care of it I could; I am sure if you will write to Mrs. Bond she will send you another copy. . . ."

I did send her a copy, and many copies, and she sang my songs for months.

During the war there were a number of pathetic cartoons and there were some amusing ones which embraced the idea of my song, or used the title as a caption. I remember one in the *Stars and Stripes* newspaper which depicted a horrible trench in which a young soldier was holding a skillet over an alcohol flame so small you could scarcely see it. In the skillet was an egg and a pathetic little piece of bacon. In his other hand was an umbrella which he held up in a futile effort to ward off a downpour of rain. Notes were flying out from under that umbrella and they were singing, "This Is the End of a Perfect Day." I could not make out the signature, but I wrote to the editor to get the name of the cartoonist, and shortly afterward I received the original drawing from this young man—a French soldier.

All the incidents connected with "The End of a Perfect Day," even in wartime, were not pathetic. One evening in Los Angeles, I was invited to a dinner given at the beach. I was a little late and as I arrived I heard the last strains of "A Perfect Day" and a great deal of good-hearted laughter. I was a little embarrassed about going in and I thought that some one had written another parody on my little song. When one has written a song, and sung it with ten or twenty thousand soldiers, one is apt, I fear, to take it a trifle seriously. When I got to the dinner everybody wanted to tell me at once what had happened. The dinner was given for an Austrian musician and composer who knew very little of America's popular music. When my song was played he stood up. When he had been standing for a few minutes some one asked him, "Why do you stand?" and he answered, "Am I the only one who stands up when your national anthem is being played?"

A few years ago I was in Jerusalem in the American Colony Home. It was a bright moonlight night and I heard the marching feet of soldiers. Soon they began singing "This Is the End of a Perfect Day." I looked out to see about twelve soldiers marching by. In the morning I said to my host, "Did you hear that music last night? Those soldiers singing?" He told me he had not. "Well," I said, "it seemed very strange, but they were singing one of my songs— 'The End of a Perfect Day.'" "Did you write that song? Will you autograph a copy for me?" "Gladly, but I have none with me," I replied. He brought out an old worn sheet of "A Perfect Day" and told me this story: Two American boys had been billeted at the American Colony Home and every evening during their stay one had played and the other had sung "The End of a Perfect Day." When they were well enough to leave they left the song as a token of their gratitude. You see, it was about all they had to give. How gladly I autographed that little song! In a few weeks word was sent to the American Colony Home that these two boys had "gone west."

I was sitting in a restaurant at Monte Carlo this last summer; I was lonely and had gone over to a table by myself quite near the orchestra. Suddenly they began playing my song. After it was finished I went to the director and asked him if he knew me. He said, "Why, no, madam." I told him I was very glad because I had written

MY FAVORITE CARTOON

TITLE PAGE OF "A PERFECT DAY," PAINTED BY MRS. BOND

Journey's End

Sung by Mr. David Bispham

A PERFECT DAY
'Cello Obligato

Words and Music by
CARRIE JACOBS-BOND

Moderato espressivo

When you come to the end of a per-fect day, And you sit a-lone with your thought, _____ While the chimes ring out with a car-ol gay, For the

S. 112-4 & 2   Med

175

The Roads of Melody

joy that the day has brought,___ Do you think what the end of a

per - fect day Can mean to a tired___ heart,___ When the

sun goes down with a flam-ing ray, And the dear friends have to part?___

Journey's End

Well, this is the end of a per - fect day, Near the end of a jour - ney,
too; But it leaves a thought that is big and strong, With a

The Roads of Melody

wish that is kind and true.____ For mem-'ry has paint-ed this

per - fect day With col - ors that nev - er fade,____ And we

find, at the end of a per-fect day, The soul of a friend we've made.____

the song and thought they were playing it for me. "We play it almost every day," he said. The incident made us both happy.

In Constantinople I was invited to a Turkish wedding and as a welcome, the gentlemen whistled the tune. They did not know the words of course.

It was played every day during the expositions at San Francisco and San Diego, and was the last music heard in the exposition grounds at San Francisco on the closing night. A great throng had gathered in the Court of Honor and as the lights were dimmed for the last time, the notes of "A Perfect Day" were heard. I was not there, but was told it was most touching.

I was in a store in Edinburgh making some purchases. When I gave the man the address for sending them to me, he asked, "Do you happen to be the Carrie Jacobs-Bond who wrote 'Poor Little Lamb'?" I answered that I was she—"and am so delighted that you did not say 'A Perfect Day.'" He replied, "Oh, I have sung that song for ten years."

One day I was at Epsom Downs on Derby Day. It was noon time and we had to stand in the cue waiting our turn to go into dinner, when I heard my song being played. I looked across the green to see a poor crippled soldier playing on a cornet. Of course, I went across to speak to him and thank him, and as I stepped out of that line three other people stepped out and followed me. They happened to be dear friends from Philadelphia, one of them being Thaddeus Rich, then the concert master of the Philharmonic Orchestra. Through that little song again came another happy day.

During that visit to England I went to see Sir James Barrie's play, "Shall We Join the Ladies?" The song was referred to three times in the play, and one verse sung. I have never met Sir James Barrie, but certainly I wanted to that evening.

I think the most impressive occasion when this song was sung was one which I missed, but my son did not. It was on the real Armistice Day. He was in New York; the town was wild with joy. He was at the Vanderbilt Hotel looking out the window, and finally he heard men singing "The End of a Perfect Day." They were forming a sort of serpentine, each man with his hands on the shoulders of the man in front, and thus they started down Fifth Avenue. Back and forth they went from the Plaza Hotel to Fifty-ninth Street, on to Washington Square.

My son joined the singing crowd and he had the exquisite joy of mingling with a hundred thousand people who were all wildly happy and above all the din thousands were joining in singing "This Is the End of a Perfect Day." I said, "Did you sing?" and he said, "No, Mother, I cried."

I now embarked upon an adventure which I had always sworn I would have have nothing to do with—that was to appear in vaudeville. I had not forgotten a certain unhappy Sunday afternoon—my first appearance in vaudeville years ago—and I knew I never should forget it. But one day, looking over papers in our safe deposit vault, I came across a contract which offered me five hundred dollars a week for appearing in vaudeville. The letter was from Milwaukee, Wisconsin. I took it immediately to my son and asked, "What in the world does this mean?" "Well, mother," he replied, "that offer came some time ago, as you will see, almost two years ago, but I never dreamed you would even consider it, and I knew you were not physically able to do such strenuous work, so I refused it. I kept the contract, however, thinking that some day I would tell you about it." I said, "Well, I am astonished; I certainly would have done it."

Immediately I hunted up the agency and made inquiry. Almost the first words the gentleman said were: "Well, Mrs. Bond, at that time we could not afford to offer you any more, but would you consider one thousand dollars a week now?" I should think I would!

"Are you the one to talk to about it?" I asked. "No," he said, "I will telegraph to Harry Weber —one of the finest managers of vaudeville artists I have ever known." And immediately reply came from Mr. Weber, asking me if I could come to New York to talk over affairs—which I did.

Almost the first thing he said to me was: "Mrs. Bond, we have chosen Helen Keller, Ernest Thompson Seton and you to start a new line of work in vaudeville and we want you to consider it seriously." It was indeed a serious thing to me, but after seeing Miss Keller and realizing

how brave she and Mrs. Macey were to undertake anything so difficult, I believed I could go
on with it. We were all novices on the stage.
Of course, Mr. Thompson Seton did not mind it
so much, but to Miss Keller and me, it was entirely a new experience.

I agreed to do it, and signed a contract for
three months. I was in very poor health, but
every consideration was shown me. I was allowed to work every other week, and so I started
out with a sweet little singer, Miss Lois Bennett,
who looked as if she might have been my little
daughter, and with a trained nurse. Of course,
the preliminary work was quite difficult for me.
My first public appearance was in a little vaudeville house in New York, on Broadway. This
theater had its greatest audience at noon. It was
really a playhouse for the workers who came in
at luncheon time. As I said before, I knew nothing about the workings of vaudeville life, and
when I was given an hour for rehearsal very early
in the morning, I was fifteen minutes late, thereby
losing my chance for a rehearsal, as every minute
was taken up until one o'clock. Part of my pro-

gram was to play "A Perfect Day" with the orchestra. I had never played with an orchestra in my life, and the thought of trying to do it without a rehearsal was more than I could stand. I telephoned to Mr. Weber and said, "I am very sorry, Mr. Weber, but I cannot go on this afternoon." "Are you ill?" "No; but I was not able to have a rehearsal." "Well, Mrs. Bond, you will have to do it, or forfeit a thousand dollars."

It is quite natural to suppose I went.

Not knowing where the stage door was, we drove up to the front entrance, and to my horror I saw in big letters CARRIE JACOBS-BOND: THE GRAND OLD LADY OF SONGDOM. I immediately forgot there had not been a rehearsal. My one thought was to find the man who wrote that sign. So into the office I went and in fury demanded to know where the manager was. A very gentle young man stepped up and said: "I did that, Mrs. Bond," and adding insult to injury, he added: "I meant it as a compliment; you know they call Gladstone—the Grand Old Man."

At that time I think Gladstone was about thirty years older than I was. Anyway, they said they would take down the sign, and they did.

Journey's End

I went back to the dressing room and everything went beautifully. I never was any more inspired to do anything in my life than I was to play with that orchestra. That was the very beginning. This we did for three days and I became accustomed to the new experience. I never had been able to make myself sing in a spotlight, with the audience in the dark, so as another kind concession, they allowed the theater to be left lighted and used a diffused light which they said made a charming effect.

My real début was made at Mt. Vernon in a lovely theater, where all the managers came to make their engagements. The work was a success from the first night.

A few years after this my son heard me telling about the "Grand Old Lady of Songdom," and he related the following story to my friends: "Yes, but the funniest part of this story was that the 'Grand Old Lady' sign had been taken off the front of the theater; but on the drop curtain, every night from that time on, just before mother's act began, the words were flashed, 'Carrie Jacobs-Bond, Grand Old Lady of Songdom,' but mother never knew it."

About the greatest thrill of all was when I sang in Washington and saw my name in electric lights for the first time, electric lights blazing down the street and reflecting on the wet pavements. I said to my nurse, "This is too much publicity; it is going to kill me." But she said that the next night I told the chauffeur to be sure to drive up to the front of the theater as I wanted to know if I had been successful enough to warrant the lights being kept on. Which goes to show how proud we are after all.

I could tell many, many stories of the experiences I went through for these three months, but they were all wonderful. Such kindness; such dear people behind the scenes. One young boy said to me, "Lady, it must be fine to begin a headliner." He went on, "I have been on the stage ever since I was a little boy and I have not arrived yet." I replied, "I have been at it for twenty-eight years and I just got in."

"Oh," he said, "that's older than I am."

"That should comfort you," I smiled.

One afternoon in Boston a frightened old lady walked into my dressing room without rapping.

I knew from her appearance she had never been in a theater before, and from her frightened looks that she thought it was the wickedest place on earth. She gave me a hurried glance from head to foot, and exclaimed, "Well, I drove forty miles to see if you looked like you sounded, and you do." From her words I knew she was satisfied with me, but felt that she should escape from that wicked place, the theater, as quickly as possible.

Once, after one of my performances in vaudeville, a sweet-faced woman came to me, and looking me in the face said, "And you don't remember me?" She said it two or three times, and the harder she looked at me the less I could recall her. Finally she said, "Don't you remember the sweet pickles?" I nearly died of embarrassment, and said: "Oh, I am so sorry I do not recall your name, but you know I have been in so many people's homes—you must remember that for twelve years I gave recitals all over this country, and was generally entertained in some one's home, and was given the most delicious food to eat. I know I praised all kinds of nice things

187

that were given to me, and I am especially fond of pickles. I assure you that I meant every word I said about them when I ate them, but I will have to say again, I do not remember, and hope you will forgive me."

She laughed, and I guess she did forgive me, because when she really thought of it, she must have known that it was quite a lapse of time to recall between the day I ate the pickles in her home and the meals that I had eaten in the twelve intervening years.

Some of the most interesting incidents of my life have come to me in speaking over the radio. I am in a position to know what damage the radio does to the song publisher, to the concert managers, to phonographs and all automatic musical instruments and even the sales of pianos. For people, some way or other, seem to think that because they can turn on the radio and get everything they want, it isn't necessary for the little girl to take music lessons any longer and they don't have to have a piano. That there are many discouraging effects of the radio all thinking people will agree, but the other side of the radio

THE PRESENT BOND SHOP, HOLLYWOOD, 1927

My Son, Frederic Jacobs Smith

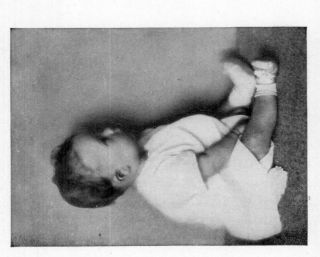

My Little Granddaughter, Betty

brings to life just such experiences as those of which I am going to tell you.

Out of the hundreds of letters I have received after doing my work on the radio, some stand out never to be forgotten, but I will only tell you of two. One was a postcard I received which said: "I am a poor old fellow and the only comfort I have ever had is the radio. No, I do not own a radio but I go to the corner drug store every evening. To-night I heard 'The Perfect Day' and I just want to thank you. God bless you." And another letter read like this: "Well, I live forty miles from nowhere on a farm, but I love my husband and children well enough to be happy here, but I used to get lonesome. To-day was a pretty hard one. It's preserving time and I put up fruit all day. First I got the children ready for school, then I canned fruit and got the meals for the workers in the field, and you know how much they can eat, and finally everybody went to bed. I still had something to do. I was fixing the tomato catsup, when I was so tired, so dead tired, I sat down and turned on the radio and the first thing I heard, 'This Is the End of a Perfect Day,' and I said, 'Well, I guess it is.' I did not burn anything and this catsup smells fine. Can you smell it? Thank you for the song."

These are the things that make you think the radio is one of the most blessed things in the world and I myself would be lost without it.

CHAPTER VI

BYPATHS

I AM not the rich woman that the world thinks I am. Perhaps if I had saved all I had earned and thought about investments and making money, and cared for money for money's sake, I might have been. But my son and Mr. Gale realized that I was rather profligate with money, and that any one who came to me with a sad story, stranger or not, would get whatever I happened to have. They begged me to allow them to give me so much a month out of my share of the Bond Shop, until a sufficient amount had been saved to guarantee enough to take care of me in my old age, that then I might take a fling. It sounded very sensible. My son took me in hand, and he has made it possible for me to have an assured income, as far as any one can be sure of anything, to take care of me in the modest way I love to live. I consider it the most sensible thing that I have ever allowed any one to do for me.

Out of this wonderful time that I've had have come great journeys. I've seen the world, oh yes, a great deal of it; and have known many, many kinds of people, and what I've spent on these journeys I consider a priceless investment.

I used to come home from Europe with hundreds of postcards tied in little packages, which I called "Little Journeys." I could see smiles on the faces of my friends; but after they had spent a few evenings with my postcards and the magic lantern they stopped smiling, and I know that many of them who have traveled as much as I, and perhaps more, have wished more than once that they had a thousand postcards and a magic lantern to remind them of the places and the wonderful things they saw.

One night at the Gamut Club (and the Gamut Club of Los Angeles, by the way, has more famous men and women members, with the exception of the Savage Club of London, than any other club in the world), they had as guests, Madame Modjeska, Fritz Kreisler, Paderewski, and two great painters, whose names I do not recall at this moment! Imagine such a galaxy for just one evening.

The Gamut Club is twenty-two years old, and Mr. Behymer, our tireless impresario, has been the president for twelve years. The smallest dues of any similar club in the world, nine dollars per year, are charged, and its greatest ambition is to give unknown, talented people a hearing and an opportunity. Every art is represented and encouraged in the Gamut Club.

One night they were entertaining Vicente Blasco Ibañez, whom we all know best as the author of *The Four Horsemen*. At the close of the evening, Mr. Behymer said, "Well, Sister Carrie, go to the piano and give us 'The End of a Perfect Day'—which it has been." I did and as I sang the song I heard another voice singing. When I went back to my seat, I said to Mr. Behymer, "Was some one singing with me?" "Yes, it was Ibañez, but he was singing the words in Spanish. Years ago he had them translated and learned the song." Naturally I was happy, and thanked this great author. The next day I received a copy of *The Four Horsemen* with a most interesting dedication in Spanish.

About two years before Luther Burbank died I had expressed the wish that I might meet him, not knowing that I was speaking to a personal friend of Mr. Burbank, and was told she would arrange a meeting. Shortly after that I received an invitation from Mr. and Mrs. Burbank, naming a time they would be glad to have me come.

I regretted it was not possible for me to go just then, for it was in the very height of the rose bloom. The time I was able to go was when his garden was filled with the most wonderful poppies I have ever seen.

I drove through Santa Rosa in the early morning—one of those rare and beautiful drives you find in northern California—reaching Mr. Burbank's modest home early in the afternoon. As I came into the parlor the first thing that caught my eye was one of my little verses on his mantel. I exclaimed, "Why, Mr. Burbank, that is one of mine!" I was so pleased to think it was in his home. He said, "Did you write that? I did not know it. Yes, it's been in my house for twelve years." These are the words:

Bypaths

It's not so much about the house,
That any one can see;
It's not so much about the ground
That calls the bird and bee.
It's just the folks that live within
And flowers that bloom without
That call the bird, and bee, and friend,
That's what we care about!

The little verse had not been signed, just the initials "C. J.-B.," and I do not suppose that he had even noticed them.

I said, "Mr. Burbank, you have given the world so much pleasure, can I do any little thing for you?" thinking that perhaps he would like to hear me sing. There was a beautiful grand piano in the room. He said, "Yes, please sing a lot of songs to me, but sing 'A Perfect Day' first."

After the little recital, he invited me to go into the garden with him. As he walked along the path through the poppies he picked one, and it seemed to me at that moment there was only one thing he thought of, or saw. Away down in the very heart of this poppy he found the tiniest little speck, and pulled it out, saying, "Yes, it's time." Then he looked at me, apologized, and said, "You see, if I could only teach some one when it's time, all the things I have worked so hard to find could be handed on. I have been offered a fine sum to go to Stanford to lecture, but, you see, Mrs. Bond, it is not possible for me to tell them how. I only know when I see it, and what I see I cannot explain."

Dear, great wonderful man! What a privilege for me to have those few hours with him! When we said good-by he invited me to come later in the year and see the field of fire plant that would be in full bloom—acres of wonderful flaming scarlet color. I intended to go, but something prevented.

When we parted I carried away with me the memory of the face of the gentlest person I had ever met, and I also carried with me Luther Burbank's complete set of books which he had autographed for me. In the last volume, in the most inconspicuous place, was the simple story of his life.

* * *

The Pasadena Tournament of Roses Association asked me if I would write the music for a prize poem for the pageant of 1926. I assented and went to Europe with the understanding that the poem would be sent to me in Paris a month or so before my return. This was the first time I had ever thought of writing music to a poem not chosen by myself, and I was very anxious, fearing that I could not do it. Time went by, but no word came. The day before I sailed the verses arrived, but no idea of music with the reading. Up to this time I had never tried to use a poem I could not sing the moment I read the words (that's what I call "listening for my inspiration"). Lovely as this poem was, I heard no tune, and after seven weary days and nights I became panicky, and for the first time in my life I knew I must write a song in a given time, and that that time was flying.

I sent for a piano and shut myself up in my room at the Pennsylvania Hotel, leaving word at the telephone desk that no one was to disturb me.

I had scarcely locked the door when I heard the little waltz which was later published. In less than half an hour it was ready for dictation, and down the hall I heard the maid humming the melody—a good sign. She had caught it by hearing me play it over and over again.

My first recital in California was given in a music school of Miss Kathyrine Cocks'. After I had finished the program my hostess said, "Please wait a moment. The children have something for you." And a hundred little children passed by, each one handing me a bunch of violets.

As I saw this line of lavender coming up the aisle, I said to myself, "This must be a very rich school. They must be bringing me a hundred dollars' worth of violets." But I took them, and was glad somebody was so rich. And they had to bring in a bushel basket to hold them all—I say "bushel basket," but it was just two market baskets which would have held a bushel. And as I went out the door a lady said to me, "You come from Chicago, and I suppose pay awful prices there for violets in the winter, but it's violet time here, and the children only pay five cents a bunch!"

That made me think, "What's the difference if you don't know the price?" They looked like a hundred dollars to me, but it wouldn't have made me any happier to know that was what they had cost.

* * *

For any one who has the appreciation of what it means to wish all one's life that you had something, having never seen the thing that you wished for, and then suddenly to find it, more beautiful than your dreams, and to live to see and own all the simple things you wanted on that spot; for those who can appreciate this, I am writing the story of my first little house.

All my life I had dreamed of a valley surrounded by great mountain peaks and away off in the distance, so far away you could not hear the beating of a wave, the wonderful ocean. Needless to say, my wishes had not been extravagant, but had they been, the spot I found to build my home upon would have met all the requirements, for it could not be bought for millions. About the house—why that is another story. I thought it could be made for $1,700, and it was. Now for the real tale.

On the road to the sea, nine miles from Los Angeles, Mrs. Anderson has made a home for travelers. They call it The Beverly Hills Hotel. One supposes a hotel to be a place where nobody cares much about you, but here you feel as if you were a special guest. It looks like home when you open the door. I lived for months in this delightful place and felt there could be nothing more lovely. But one fine day some friends of mine who knew and loved the whole of California, said:

"Yes, of course, this is a lovely place, but have you ever motored slowly along through southern California?"

I had to admit I never had.

The invitation they gave me was quickly accepted and the day was set. We started in the early morning and drove to Elysian Park, a park perfect before the hand of man had touched it.

The drive to the highest point was six hundred feet. My friends said: "Now, we will start from here," and we did.

We drove down and down through wooded

200

hills and sunny spots for a quiet ten miles and finally found ourselves in Pasadena, truly the garden spot—orange trees, rose gardens, great arroyos, and then grandest of all, snow-capped Mt. Lowe. It was beyond expression in words.

Then we drove about forty miles through orange, lemon, olive and walnut groves, acres and acres of vineyard, and at the end of this came to Riverside; Riverside, with its House Beautiful, the lovely Mission Inn, where every new guest finds himself in a dear, quaint little room (or large, according to his pocketbook). But no matter about the pocketbooks, the basket of oranges is just as large in the little room, and the bouquet that somebody brings you about a minute after you arrive makes you feel as though you had just got home.

The next morning we were up with the sun and drove to the top of a mountain called Rubidoux and here, for the first time in my life, I saw a valley *something* like my dream, but there was no ocean. I still said to myself: "But maybe there is one somewhere."

The next day we rode to Redlands, where everybody's house seemed more beautiful than everybody else's. They are all built on wonderful hillsides where it looks as though every kind of tree in the world grew. Ivy-covered banks with tree trunks and branches festooned with their lovely vines, and gold of Ophir roses, hedges of them, eight and ten feet high, and one in particular a half mile long bordering one side of the Smiley Heights garden. Truly, I felt that I was driving through Arcadia.

Of course, people do work in Redlands, but it all seems like play to me. To be able to work out-of-doors all winter in this balmy atmosphere, with the perfume of the orange blossoms always in the air, would seem like a yearly picnic to those who live "back East."

There are so many beautiful things between Los Angeles and the place I am going to tell you about that we will just skip along and stop but an hour at the old Mission of San Juan Capistrano. It would be too long a story for me to explain to those who have never been through California the meaning of these old ruins. Suffice it to say that to the heart of every one who has ever lived in California these old missions are precious.

Now for about fifteen miles we drove along a most beautiful road on the ocean beach and the first thing we knew we were at the foot of a mountain that seemed perpendicular, but it wasn't. We just put on a little more steam and flew right up the side of the mountain and then we stopped and gasped for breath, for we were on the mesa and there before us stood the famous Torrey Pines that have weathered the ocean storms for no one knows how many years.

The beauty of this scene could not be fully grasped. It took some time to realize all we saw. Below us, I should say about five miles, was La Jolla, a lovely quiet spot with its remarkable cove, its caves and the mysterious White Lady, and high up on the banks the most unusual little houses, built by Mrs. Heinrich; and on beyond all this, San Diego, with its Point Loma; Coronado with its tented beach; the great protected bay; the grand Pacific Ocean with its Mexican Islands all gleaming in the sun.

When we got to San Diego I met two people, who later in my life became very near and dear to me—Colonel and Mrs. Ed Fletcher—and they took us for a little journey to a place called Grossmont. This little mountain is owned by Mr. Fletcher and was one of his dreams for which he was often laughed at, but twenty years ago I heard him say, "Some day there will be a theater upon that Helix mountain and, Mrs. Bond, you will look right down into a lake from your lot." People smiled, but we have the theater on the top of Helix which seats six thousand people, one of the most beautiful things that I have ever seen, and I do look down into a beautiful lake from the east room. So, after all, it doesn't pay to laugh at a dreamer, especially a practical dreamer, for they are the people who make the world beautiful.

Well, once more we took a long breath and started to the top of the mountain called Grossmont. We traveled around and around its sides, first up and then down, then around again, coming up several hundred feet, and finally reached the summit and faced the ocean!

How can I tell you of the glories of that sunset! I hope some of my readers have the proper imagination. Think of the most beautiful colors you have seen in all your life. Well, that is about one half as beautiful as this was. Tears were in my eyes and I turned and said: "Well, here is my spot! The only place in the world I have ever wanted to live."

To make a long story short, that spot was for sale. I had money enough to buy it, and I did. We drove home. My friends thought I had lost my senses. For four years I built a house every day on that spot—all in my mind, of course, because I had to earn the money first. But one great day I had saved enough so I took the journey again and with a string and a few stones and sticks I measured out the distance of my first mountain home.

It had a room forty by twenty-nine feet, because that was the space between the boulders. Then on each end where there seemed to be a vacancy big enough for a room I added one. There are two lean-tos in my home. I then called in Messrs. Davis and Brennan, contractors, from La Mesa, who did the rest.

On one side it greets the sunrise; the other, with a great smiling porch, looks down on the sunset. Then, of course, there had to be a few windows. So in the little room that measures forty by twenty-nine I put twenty sliding windows. The wicker furniture is painted the soft green-gray of eucalyptus leaves; the cretonnes have the soft pinks, yellows and lavender of its bark, and in the big eucalyptus-green tiled fireplace we burn big eucalyptus logs. We spur it on sometimes with a stick of orange wood, to make it sound extravagant, and then we dream.

The house boasts all the modern improvements —water, gas and electricity; but when we have company we sit in the candlelight.

All we have to do in this little place to bring ourselves back to real life is to look down into the green and brown valley of El Cajon, with its little towns scattered here and there, where the train comes and goes sixteen times a day. We do not hear the wheels nor smell the smoke, but in about fifteen minutes' walk we can take the train to San Diego.

When you come to my little mansion you drive with Mr. Jones behind a tame old horse of twenty-four summers, in a comfortable old two-seated wagon. When you journey this way you have some opportunity to make yourself familiar with the scenery, as the drive is about thirty minutes long. If you like to travel as some people do—as fast as possible—and if you have good nerves and are absolutely without fear of a sharp curve, you can come up by motor in about ten minutes.

We did not blast any of the beautiful rocks, and my home nestles between those beautiful stones. I call it "Nest-o'-Rest," and have written a little song to it, naming it, "A Cottage in God's Garden":

I've a cottage in God's garden, upon a mountain
*   high,*
Away from strife and turmoil, and all life's din
*   and cry,*
Away from care and sorrow and all earth's tears
*   and woe,*
A cottage in God's garden where I am free to go.

There's a cottage in God's garden where my tired
*   feet may rest,*
And weary though my soul be, my spirit there
*   is blest,*
The wild birds chant their carol, and wild flowers
*   bloom galore*
Out in God's lovely garden. How could I ask
*   for more?*

The Roads of Melody

On the hill across the way, which is two thousand feet high, Mrs. White has built the Helix theater of which I have spoken and dedicated it to the memory of her beloved mother.

Josef Hofmann called on me one day. I had been told of his wonderful home on the side of the mountain looking into Lake Geneva, and he said, "This is more like the situation of my own home than anything I have ever seen, but, even if you have not the great lake you have something else I think perhaps is better. You can work by yourself up here; you would never have to think that you were disturbing some one. Where my house is situated we have quite near neighbors."

I have neighbors on Grossmont, but we are really quite a way apart. My home is so by itself that if I did practice six hours a day it would not be near enough to any one's home to disturb him.

When I first came to Grossmont, I was almost overcome with the beauty outdoors. The flowers, trees, mountains and ocean, everything that is beautiful seemed to be here. And so when I built my home on the top of the mountain, I decided to have an art gallery and so I built my windows as if they were picture frames and looking outdoors was visiting the art gallery. In this art gallery I have a magnificent collection, but it is not a private collection. The pictures are for every one who will look. Pictures have always been an inspiration in writing music and when I discovered the myriad of pictures that I might frame here at Grossmont, just with some lumber and panes of glass, I determined to make it in fact what it is in name, a "Nest-o'-Rest." Here I come every year, with a dear friend or two and Tom, my sweet-voiced canary, and my faithful dogs, Mike and Pooch, to rest and to seek from the sky and the mountains and the rocks the relation of life to the songs I would sing, and I find it here, even as I find the physical rebuilding also.

My pictures are all painted by the Great Master. They are painted for all time and no thief can break in and steal them, no marauding fire or storm destroy them. They are painted to last forever and they grow fresher in color and more vivid in their glowing tints whenever the

great water-color painter, Rain, comes along to
restore their bright hues.

*   *   *

About the Bond Shop in Hollywood. That
was a dream that came true. From the time I
had the first little Bond Shop in the hall bedroom, the idea was in my mind of a lovely little
English building with the sign "Bond Shop" over
the door. Inside there would be a nice little
fireplace, and probably a counter with cases for the
sheets of music back of it; on one side of the counter there would be a little grilled door which
opened on to stairs that carried one up to a little
duplex room that would be my private office. I
just wanted to feel I had an office—I had no need
of one, for my son had always done the real
business of the Bond Shop—but this office I really
wanted. Downstairs, back of the Bond Shop,
there would be a very fine office for my son; lovely
old furniture, and a dear little spinet would dec-
orate the Bond Shop proper; and there would be
great space in the back of the store for the stock
and the wrapping rooms, and all the necessary
things.

Well, it came to pass, and we moved everything from Chicago to beautiful Hollywood, and I saw my dream come true. But, alas, within three months the publishers found so much fault with our having the supply so far from the demand that we finally agreed to Mr. Gustav Schirmer's proposition to take over the publication and distribution of the Bond compositions, and he carried them to Boston. His splendid interest and coöperation has continued these many years, God bless him!

I know I have an office although I seldom see it—I love home too much—and I know there is a sign on a building on Highland Avenue which says, "The Bond Shop," just a stone's throw from the magnificent Hollywood Bowl where each summer we sit with thousands of music lovers listening to "The Symphonies Under the Stars"; and near that hallowed open theater where "The Christ Play," written by the late Christine Witherell Stevenson, is so beautifully produced each season.

* * *

The Roads of Melody

Many, many people ask me this question, "What can I do with myself?" That always seems a foolish question to me for how can anybody tell others what to do with themselves, *if they don't know?* It's hard enough to try to tell them *how,* after they know *what* in the first place. The worth-while people generally have an idea of what they'd like to do, and I should say to them, "If you have a gift, even a little one, begin; and if you have a gift big enough for somebody else to see, work harder than ever. But don't desire to be an opera singer if you have no ear for music, nor want to be an artist if you're color blind." But most of us know some people who really wish to do the impossible. I always knew I wanted to be a song writer. I had the talent but I had to work. I was advised by some one who did not know me, and yet was a blood relation, to be a designer, to study to be a dressmaker—but I never asked anybody what I should do. I knew my greatest gift. But what I didn't know was the terrible difficulties that lay before me to make it earn our living. If I had known that for years I must walk over a road filled with stones and stubble and that I

My Son and I as We Started Out Together.
He Was Twelve.

CARRIE JACOBS-BOND

should have to water it with tears to lay the dust I was constantly making (I don't mean real tears, but aches of my throat which kept the tears from flowing), I wonder if I would have kept on walking.

You see, I traveled on almost every other road before I found the sign marked "Road to Song Land," and I often wonder why I never gave up, but I never *thought* of giving up in my life. Only once did I think I was lost and that was finally when I was too ill to go down town again to wait once more outside some one's door where I had been told to "come the next day," only to hear the words, "Sorry, but you'll have to come tomorrow. Busy." And I had spent almost my last dime to go. But I know now people didn't mean to be cruel; they probably never guessed how poor I was; I never looked shabby. I had learned to turn my old dress inside out; had learned how to put a damp cloth over a hot flat iron and steam a piece of old velvet so it looked almost new; learned never to cut a piece to trim a hat if it could be utilized later for a belt; learned how to revive a tired ostrich feather with the dull side of a knife—all these things kind poverty had

213

taught me, and I used some of my knowledge every day.

I often wonder why people with talent refuse to play or sing for others. If some one asked them why they had been given a talent, the honest answer would be, "to use," and if they were generous as they should be in their appreciation of the gift, they would be glad to give it when they were asked. A talent is generally rewarded. I mean, after one has learned to do anything well people pay gladly to hear it or see it. But what a difference in audiences. The enthusiastic demonstrations of the Europeans! But we Americans are learning to show our joy and we are fast learning the little trick of how to get something. The sure way of getting something is to be willing to give something—so the more the applause, the better the artist works.

A few years ago I often took with me a young girl to hear some of our very finest programs. And I would applaud until it seemed my hands hurt, but my friend would sit placidly with her hands folded. Finally one day I said, "Don't you enjoy this?" and she said, "Oh, yes, very much." And I said, "Well, if everybody expressed it in the manner you do, I don't believe the artist would play again!" And she said, "I never thought of that." How strange never to think of saying "thank you" when something beautiful is given you! But from that time on, she was different.

I will say that many, many times I have wished I could sit and listen in silence, in the dark, until the last number, and then say, with the most wonderful applause, how really great it had all been. But that isn't being done. That's something that is going to happen to me when I get to Heaven— a wonderful place to sit in perfect silence, with a dim light, to listen to my heart's content to beautiful music; and the artist will know, *without applause,* how deeply touched I am. That would rest my soul.

When I wandered into the office of Amber in Chicago on that eventful day when I had my first newspaper interview, after our afternoon of visiting, she gave me one of her little books called *A String of Amber Beads.* On the flyleaf she had written, "To a dear tramp who came in one day to leave a song, but stole my heart." My first, and best beloved book.

I think next to that as a treasure in books, are the three which were given me by James Whitcomb Riley—in one of which he had written, "Little children's always good, if they's only understood."

The finest compliment I ever had paid me was from Reverend Robert J. Burdette who called me, "Riley in Petticoats."

*　　*　　*

Years ago in a theater in Chicago I was surprised by finding I had been seated next to a very dear friend who introduced me to one of her friends. And as we left the theater, my old friend said, "That is Mrs. H——, a wealthy woman from New York, who has been very much interested in your songs, and now that she has met you, wishes to call on you. Whatever she wants to do for you will be done from the depth of a generous, helpful heart, and you accept it." I said, "Ask her if she will come to see me tomorrow morning." So the invitation was accepted and about ten o'clock the new friend came.

Our street was torn up, so she had to leave her taxicab a block away. Well, we had a wonderful talk and the first thing I knew, it was twelve o'clock. I was living very simply, but, of course, things were better than they had been, and in my kitchen was a dear old colored woman, Nancy, who was in her younger days, the original "Aunt Jemima Pancake-Maker." I think she was one hundred years old; anyway she was very, very old, and did not know how many years she had lived, but she loved and cared for my son and me.

Rather apologetically I said, "I would love to have you stay for lunch if you do not mind the style we live in." She stayed until about four o'clock in the afternoon, when with an exclamation that startled me she said, "Great Heavens, I left a taxicab down here at the corner. What do you suppose it's going to cost?" She told me years afterwards that it cost twenty-nine dollars.

* * *

During the lean years it was great fun (you know you must have fun once in a while even if you are poor and in trouble, if you want anybody to like you and you want to keep on living)

217

to invite a friend for a meal and then begin to get it as I did with the words, "If you'll excuse me I'll get dinner." Then I would step on the piano stool and pull up a one-burner gas stove by its left leg to which I had tied a strong string. The piano had to be set crosswise to give the stove a chance for connection, because the only low gas connection in the room was in the baseboard back of the piano. Before the surprised visitor could guess what was happening I would go to the lower part of the wash basin cupboard and produce the tin oven and cooking pans. Then from underneath the lounge I would pull a folding card table and begin preparing the food. The coffee was made first and kept hot on top of the oven while the food was cooking.

It was very easy to cook three things at once (provided I had them) but the coffee was a question until I discovered it was all right to keep it hot on top and then warm it up as soon as the oven was taken off the burner. Strange how everybody enjoyed those meals! I sometimes think I would like to do it all again, but just for amusement.

I wonder what the world would be like if there

were nobody to do the simple things! I wonder how folks would get along without snappers, and hooks and eyes, and pins. Nothing could be much commoner than they are, but they fill a very much needed place. You see, lots of folks can get along without a point lace collar, but I should hate to see folks try to get along without the other commodities I've spoken of. And sometimes songs (simple songs) like pins keep folks together.

*   *   *

My story would not be complete without a little account of the life of my son and me. He was always my companion and we always had a perfect understanding. Many people think we are much alike; I only wish we were. I should like to have more of his qualities. He was born with helpful heart and hands, always wanted to be of service when he was a little child, and was one of those children whom the neighbors like to have come in. It was never any trouble to find a place for him to spend the afternoon and it was perfectly natural, when he was told that Dr. Bond had gone and his mother was left alone in the world, that he should put his arms around her and say, "Mother, darling, I could do something for you. I could be as kind as doctor always was, and I always will be," and so from his ninth year we walked hand in hand.

All those struggling years in Chicago, when I had to leave him evening after evening to give recitals, and he had worked hard all day himself and studied after he came home, I never found him in bed upon my return. He might be sound asleep, but he would be sitting up, waiting for his mother. He always had some sort of refreshments, if nothing more than a dainty sandwich of bread and butter and everything ready to make mother a cup of hot coffee as soon as she came in.

He learned to cook so that he could help me and he often laughingly said that by being a chef he was more than once let out of a hard job by promising to stay in camp and make baking-powder biscuits for the crowd.

He tried to learn to iron. It was at the time men and boys were wearing stiff shirts. I came home one afternoon to find him attempting to do up his shirt. Of course, the first touch of the flatiron on the starched bosom made a brown mark, which he was busy rubbing off as I came in. Another time, when he was trying to save all the money he could to send to mother, he decided to wash out his linens and undergarments. That night after he came in from his work he did his washing, hanging it over all the furniture in the room, only to find the next morning that the wet clothing had taken the varnish off everything, and it cost twenty-five dollars to have it refinished. It was quite an expensive laundry bill, and after this second experience with washing and ironing he gave up the laundry business.

At seventeen I asked him to go into business with me. This he did gladly and willingly. I was always his first consideration, and I did not know until many years afterwards that the desire of his life had been to be a physician, but he had never mentioned this to me. He just went on being a music publisher, and we have carried on together for thirty years.

Below are two little poems that I wrote for him which he has framed and hanging by his desk:

The Roads of Melody

A gift for you, my darling Son,
A gift for golden years,
A mother's gift of care supreme,
Beyond this vale of tears.

A gift of golden love, my Boy,
That you have given me,
A golden gift of forty years,
That's kept me young and free.

A gift for golden truth, my Boy,
That's kept me strong and true,
And here's another gift, my Boy,
Your Mother's love for you.

TO MY SON

So many years have come and gone
Since first you came to me,
That, as I look back, there's a mist,
Yet through it I can see,
A little Baby's wondrous face,
Can touch a baby's hand;
And feel a little beating heart
My own can understand.
I wonder if you really know
You've been the world to me,
Through every moment of my life

Bypaths

Yours is the face I see:
That every joy you've ever known,
And every sorrow, too,
Has touched the very soul of me,
For I am part of you.
And now I know in all this world
That I can never find
A Son more gentle or more true,
And no one half so kind.
You helped me bear my burdens well
Through glorious struggling years;
'Twas you who brought me happy days
And wiped away my tears.
All this is what I think of you
(No matter what I say).
So Dear God, bless my only Son,
On this, his own birthday.

They do not say half I wanted to say, but everybody who has a child in this world knows the great joy, or the great sorrow, that they can bring, and mine has brought me only comfort.

It is too bad children do not know before it is too late what the love of a good mother and father is. One often hears it said, "Oh, yes, but see what a mother he had," or "See what parents he had." This is not a true thing to say;

223

I have known some of the most wonderful mothers and fathers to have children who have broken their hearts, and I have known some wonderful children who had mothers and fathers that disgraced them. No, it is not always so, but the chances are ten to one that a good mother can pretty nearly make a good child. The first thing to do is to get the confidence of your child, and the next thing is to keep it, and love, being the greatest thing in the world, is the best thing to begin with—unselfish love tempered with good judgment.

(1)

THE END